Norman Bethune

Norman Bethune
by ADRIENNE CLARKSON

With an Introduction by
John Ralston Saul
SERIES EDITOR

PENGUIN CANADA

Published by the Penguin Group

Penguin Group (Canada), 90 Eglinton Avenue East, Suite 700, Toronto, Ontario, Canada M4P 2Y3
(a division of Pearson Canada Inc.)

Penguin Group (USA) Inc., 375 Hudson Street, New York, New York 10014, U.S.A.
Penguin Books Ltd, 80 Strand, London WC2R 0RL, England
Penguin Ireland, 25 St Stephen's Green, Dublin 2, Ireland (a division of Penguin Books Ltd)
Penguin Group (Australia), 250 Camberwell Road, Camberwell, Victoria 3124, Australia
(a division of Pearson Australia Group Pty Ltd)
Penguin Books India Pvt Ltd, 11 Community Centre, Panchsheel Park,
New Delhi – 110 017, India
Penguin Group (NZ), 67 Apollo Drive, Rosedale, North Shore 0745, Auckland, New Zealand
(a division of Pearson New Zealand Ltd)
Penguin Books (South Africa) (Pty) Ltd, 24 Sturdee Avenue, Rosebank,
Johannesburg 2196, South Africa

Penguin Books Ltd, Registered Offices: 80 Strand, London WC2R 0RL, England

First published 2009
1 2 3 4 5 6 7 8 9 10   (RRD)

LIBRARY AND ARCHIVES CANADA CATALOGUING IN PUBLICATION

Clarkson, Adrienne, 1939-
Norman Bethune / Adrienne Clarkson.

(Extraordinary Canadians)
ISBN 978-0-670-06731-2

1. Bethune, Norman, 1890-1939. 2. Surgeons—Canada—Biography.
I. Title. II. Series: Extraordinary Canadians
R464.B4 C53 2009   617.092   C2009-900467-4

Visit the Penguin Group (Canada) website at **www.penguin.ca**

Special and corporate bulk purchase rates available; please see
www.penguin.ca/corporatesales or call 1-800-810-3104, ext. 477 or 474

This book was printed on 30% PCW recycled paper

For Walter B. Mann, 1910–1995,
my English teacher at Lisgar Collegiate Institute,
from whom I first heard of Norman Bethune
and who encouraged me
"to strive, to seek, to find, and not to yield."

CONTENTS

John Ralston Saul

How do civilizations imagine themselves? One way is for each of us to look at ourselves through our society's most remarkable figures. I'm not talking about hero worship or political iconography. That is a danger to be avoided at all costs. And yet people in every country do keep on going back to the most important people in their past.

This series of Extraordinary Canadians brings together rebels, reformers, martyrs, writers, painters, thinkers, political leaders. Why? What is it that makes them relevant to us so long after their deaths?

For one thing, their contributions are there before us, like the building blocks of our society. More important than that are their convictions and drive, their sense of what is right and wrong, their willingness to risk all, whether it be their lives, their reputations, or simply being wrong in public. Their ideas, their triumphs and failures, all of these somehow constitute a mirror of our society. We look at these people, all dead, and discover what we have been, but also what we can be. A mirror is an instrument for measuring ourselves. What we see can be both a warning and an encouragement.

These eighteen biographies of twenty key Canadians are centred on the meaning of each of their lives. Each of them is very different, but these are not randomly chosen great figures. Together they produce a grand sweep of the creation of modern Canada, from our first steps as a democracy in 1848 to our questioning of modernity late in the twentieth century.

All of them except one were highly visible on the cutting edge of their day while still in their twenties, thirties, and forties. They were young, driven, curious. An astonishing level of fresh energy surrounded them and still does. We in the twenty-first century talk endlessly of youth, but power today is often controlled by people who fear the sort of risks and innovations embraced by everyone in this series. A number of them were dead—hanged, infected on a battlefield, broken by their exertions—well before middle age. Others hung on into old age, often profoundly dissatisfied with themselves.

Each one of these people has changed you. In some cases you know this already. In others you will discover how through these portraits. They changed the way the world hears music, thinks of war, communicates. They changed how each of us sees what surrounds us, how minorities are treated, how we think of immigrants, how we look after each other, how we imagine ourselves through what are now our stories.

You will notice that many of them were people of the word. Not just the writers. Why? Because civilizations are built around many themes, but they require a shared public language. So Laurier, Bethune, Douglas, Riel, LaFontaine, McClung, Trudeau, Lévesque, Big Bear, even Carr and Gould, were masters of the power of language. Beaverbrook was one of the most powerful newspaper publishers of his day. Countries need action and laws and courage. But civilization is not a collection of prime ministers. Words, words, words—it is around these that civilizations create and imagine themselves.

The authors I have chosen for each subject are not the obvious experts. They are imaginative, questioning minds from among our leading writers and activists. They have, each one of them, a powerful connection to their subject. And in their own lives, each is engaged in building what Canada is now becoming.

That is why a documentary is being filmed around each subject. Images are yet another way to get at each subject and to understand their effect on us.

The one continuous, essential voice of biography since 1961 has been the *Dictionary of Canadian Biography*. But there has not been a project of book-length biographies such as Extraordinary Canadians in a hundred years, not since the Makers of Canada series. And yet every generation understands the past differently, and so sees in the mirror of these remarkable figures somewhat different lessons. As history rolls on, some truths remain the same while others are revealed in a new and unexpected way.

What strikes me again and again is just how dramatically ethical decisions figured in these people's lives. They form the backbone of history and memory. Some of them, Big Bear, for example, or Dumont, or even Lucy Maud Montgomery, thought of themselves as failures by the end of their lives. But the ethical cord that was strung taut through their work has now carried them on to a new meaning and even greater strength, long after their deaths.

Each of these stories is a revelation of the tough choices unusual people must make to find their way. And each of us as readers will find in the desperation of the Chinese revolution, the search for truth in fiction, the political and military dramas, different meanings that strike a personal chord. At first it is that personal emotive link to such figures which draws us in. Then we find they are a key that opens the whole society of their time to us. Then we realize that in that 150-year period many of them knew each other, were friends, opposed each other. Finally, when all these stories are put together, you will see that a whole new debate has been created around Canadian civilization and the shape of our continuous experiment.

Norman Bethune is perhaps the most extreme and uncompromising example we have of an ethical leader. His drive led him from working for Canada's poor to the Spanish Civil War to the cause of Mao Zedong in China. There, with his death, he became the Chinese model for the ideal foreigner. And yet for Canadians today that model is not esoteric. Bethune carried an idea of the public good that cannot be limited to any particular political movement or country. His life represents an unrelenting personal commitment to individual people in a way that gives meaning to internationalism. Adrienne Clarkson reveals the shape of his ideals, his views of love, his genius as a doctor, and his relentless drive to serve and change the world, even if it cost him his life.

CHAPTER ONE

A Man Who Is of Value to the People

In the middle of a guerrilla war in China, the stretcher-bearers carrying him across the mountains in search of help paused while Dr. Norman Bethune wrote this letter:

> I came back from the front yesterday. There was no good in my being there. I couldn't get out of bed or operate.... Had uncontrolled chills and fever all day [on November 8]. Temp. around 39.6 C., bad. Gave instructions I was to be informed of any abdominal cases of fractured femur or skull cases.... Next day (9th), more vomiting all day, high fever. Next day (10th) regiment commander (3rd Regiment) instructed I be sent back, useless for work. Vomiting on stretcher all the day. High fever, over 40 C. I think I have either septicaemia from the gangrenous fever or typhus fever. Can't get to sleep, mentally very

bright. Phenacitin and aspirin, woven's powder, antipyrine, caffeine, all useless.

Dr. Ch'en arrived here today. If my stomach settles down will return to Hua Pai Hospital tomorrow. Very rough road over mountain pass.

I feel freely today. Pain over heart—water 120–130°. Will see you tomorrow, I expect.

Bethune died at approximately five o'clock the next morning, November 12, 1939. He was forty-nine years old. This lonely death, in a filthy, war-torn village, surrounded by people with whom he could not directly speak, seems impossibly far from the distinction he would later achieve as the single most famous Canadian in the world, known to a billion and a half Chinese.

This last letter is infused with Bethune's determination to continue, despite everything, with Mao Zedong's Eighth Route Army as it desperately fought on against the Japanese invaders. It was just three years after the Long March.

The founding myth of Communist China originates in the Long March. In 1934, Mao Zedong and the Communists had been driven out of their strongholds in the southeast by Chiang Kai-shek's Chinese Nationalist Party (the Kuomintang). After two years of incredible endurance and defiance, fighting their way across five thousand miles, they reached the Yellow Plateau and the caves of Yan'an in northwest China. Of the one hundred thousand who set out, only twenty thousand remained. A year later, in March 1938, Dr. Norman Bethune arrived with two other foreigners to join the Communists as they turned their attention from the civil war against the Nationalist Party to repelling the Japanese invasion. Bethune was there for just under twenty months, but during that time his exploits achieved the same mythic proportions as the Long March.

The Bethune Museum in Shijiazhuang, China, preserves all his sacred relics: the portable typewriter from which poured newspaper articles, letters, reports, and medical texts—a huge volume of material from someone who was most often alone as the only foreign doctor among thirteen million Chinese; the box for medical supplies fitted to be carried on a saddle; his stethoscope, his watch, and a blood pressure gauge. The museum is spotless, airy, and modern. Chinese tourists move around, murmuring respectfully to one another. Bethune is venerated by the Chinese, and he loved them. China was his apotheosis. The Chinese understood him: his impatience they loved as unlimited eagerness, his stubbornness as unequivocal determination, and his dominance as unshakeable commitment. He found within himself a deeply humane and sustained response to Chinese suffering, determination, and courage. His compassion made him heedless of himself; he was tender with the weak, and his heart was, if anything, too open and ripe for bruising.

LIKE ULYSSES, Norman Bethune lived his life driven by the journey itself, not to achieve its end. The search to him was everything.

Political philosopher Stanley Ryerson, who was in Bethune's Marxist study group in Montreal in 1934–35, relates that the group read Georgiy Plekhanov's "On the Role of the Individual in History." Plekhanov's discussion of freedom and necessity would have intrigued Bethune, whose mind had been formed by the Presbyterian doctrine of predestination and hellfire. He was already working with his Montreal medical group on public health, and he certainly would not have been unstirred by Plekhanov's declaration that

> until the individual has won freedom by heroic effort in philosophical thinking, he does not fully belong to himself and his mental tortures are the shameful tribute he pays to external necessity which stands opposed to him. But as soon as this individual throws off the yoke of this painful and

shameful restriction, he is born for a new, full and hitherto never experienced life; *and his free actions become the conscious and free expression of necessity* [emphasis mine]. Then he will become a great social force; and then nothing can, and nothing will, prevent him from "bursting on cunning falsehood like a storm of wrath divine."

Plekhanov quotes Bismarck, who stated the contrary view that "we cannot make history: we must wait while it is being made. We will not make fruit ripen more quickly by subjecting it to the heat of a lamp; and if we pluck the fruit before it is ripe, we will only prevent its growth and spoil it."

In other words, individuals operating in history can never change everything. But Bethune must have wondered what kind of influence he could have on the events that he saw as important while serving medical needs. That he had earlier contributed innovative skills as a doctor for the Republican forces opposing fascism during the Spanish Civil War— before the Mackenzie-Papineau Battalion of Canadian volunteers even got organized—or that he focused on China so quickly after returning from Spain resulted from his intuitive sense that he was acting in the direct historical moment. In neither case was he behaving as though he were going to change events militarily. He inserted himself as he could into the events and did what he could. He was a fine doctor, and he realized that it was through medicine that he would be able to help in the struggles of others.

Mao Zedong, then a young revolutionary leader who would eventually change world history, eulogized Bethune the month after his death as the great foreigner who showed the Chinese the way to true internationalism. These are the only words Mao Zedong ever wrote about a foreigner. Mao mentions that he met Bethune just once, and yet the Chinese leader was able to make very clear the significance of this dead Canadian. The message about Bethune Mao conveyed to the Chinese people does not depend on personal friendship but on an appreciation of the practical and symbolic role Bethune played in Chinese history. Mao's words were memorized by all Chinese schoolchildren for decades, and almost every adult could launch into the eulogy at any moment.

> Comrade Norman Bethune, a member of the Communist Party of Canada, was around fifty when he was sent by the Communist Parties of Canada and the United States to China; he made light of travelling thousands of miles to help us in

our War of Resistance Against Japan. He arrived in Yenan in the spring of last year, went to work in the Wutai Mountains, and to our great sorrow died a martyr at his post. What kind of spirit is this that makes a foreigner selflessly adopt the cause of the Chinese people's liberation as his own? It is the spirit of internationalism, the spirit of communism, from which every Chinese Communist must learn. Leninism teaches that the world revolution can only succeed if the proletariat of the capitalist countries supports the struggle for liberation of the colonial and semi-colonial peoples and if the proletariat of the colonies and semi-colonies supports that of the proletariat of the capitalist countries. Comrade Bethune put this Leninist line into practice. We Chinese Communists must also follow this line in our practice. We must unite with the proletariat of all the capitalist countries … for this is the only way to overthrow imperialism, to liberate our nation and people and to liberate the other nations and peoples of the world. This is our internationalism, the internationalism with which we oppose both narrow nationalism and narrow patriotism.

Comrade Bethune's spirit, his utter devotion to others without any thought of self, was shown in his great sense of responsibility in his work and his great warm-heartedness towards all comrades and the people. Every Communist must learn from him.... No one who returned from the front failed to express admiration for Bethune whenever his name was mentioned, and none remained unmoved by his spirit. In the Shansi-Chahar-Hopei border area, no soldier or civilian was unmoved who had been treated by Dr. Bethune or had seen how he worked. Every Communist must learn this true communist spirit from Comrade Bethune.

Comrade Bethune was a doctor, the art of healing was his profession and he was constantly perfecting his skill, which stood very high in the Eighth Route Army's medical service. His example is an excellent lesson for those people who wish to change their work the moment they see something different and for those who despise technical work as of no consequence or as promising no future.

Comrade Bethune and I met only once. Afterwards he wrote me many letters. But I was busy, and I wrote him only one letter and do not even know if he ever received it. I am deeply grieved over his death. Now we are all commemorating him, which shows how profoundly his spirit inspires everyone. We must all learn the spirit of absolute selflessness from him. With this spirit everyone can be very useful to the people. A man's ability may be great or small, but if he has this spirit, he is already noble-minded and pure, a man of moral integrity and above vulgar interests, a man who is of value to the people.

Mao gives the sense that Bethune behaved as he did because he could not behave in any other way. The idea of the individual becoming a great social force is embodied in his tribute. In singling out Bethune in this way, he is talking about how, even in a collective movement like Communism, individuals make history.

Bethune went to China because of his beliefs: he hated fascism and decided to help the Chinese in their struggle against the Japanese. Two years before, in 1936, he went to Spain because he believed that the legally elected Republic was being crushed not just by fascism from within but by the larger movement of fascism in Germany and Italy, which was aiding

General Franco, the Spanish leader of the military coup. Bethune never claimed anything in abstract or symbolic terms; reality was his guide, and he followed it ruthlessly.

Mao places emphasis on Bethune's warmth, selflessness, integrity, and internationalism in an attempt to use him in a character-building exercise for the Chinese people. He would not have expected his tribute to gain him anything in the Western world. He wasn't looking for foreign aid. He simply wanted to pay tribute to what the Chinese thought was so remarkable—that a man from Canada could come and give himself totally to their cause to the extent of dying for it.

Bethune was an example of somebody who, by the sudden decision of his will, could introduce into the course of events a new, unexpected, and transforming force. We will never know how important he really was to the victory of the Chinese Revolution, except that he organized a medical system suitable to a guerrilla army, wrote dozens of medical manuals, trained peasants to be paramedicals—who functioned, in effect, as nurses and doctors—all the while saving countless lives on improvised operating tables at the front lines, which he travelled on horseback or on foot. He became one of those individual human forces who communicate to others the possibility of victory even in hopeless conditions. We can state with some certainty that he saved hundreds of lives with his blood transfusion service in Spain, but what that contributed to the Republic apart from sheer humanitarian value would be difficult to ascertain. After all, the Republicans lost and Franco triumphed. Interestingly enough, Bethune fulfilled a condition that Plekhanov states must be present in order for the individual to influence history—that the existing social order "must not bar the road to the person possessing the talent which is needed and useful precisely at the given time." Bethune possessed medical knowledge to a very high degree, and even though transfusion was not his specialty, he had the right background to understand it when he made up his mind that he was going to develop it in the field in Spain in 1936–37.

Bethune became a social force because that was the role he chose to play, initially as a medical student working for Frontier College with illiterate immigrant labourers in lumber camps, and later as a young doctor in Montreal working with poor, marginalized youth in the Children's Art Group and with the Montreal Group for the Security of the People's Health. And though he could not change outcomes, his talents allowed him to change certain features of events.

His painting and his writing made him feel he was an artist. He was not philosophically or intellectually a person who would have become a Marxist political figure. Had he not died in China—and returned instead to Canada—it is difficult to imagine him as a Communist in the sense that Fred Rose, Tim Buck, and other of his contemporaries were. What would he have done in 1939? Perhaps he would have joined the Royal Canadian Medical Corps and gone overseas to continue fighting fascism, and from there gone on to the next cause he could believe in.

In his two intersections with world history, in Spain and in China, Bethune seemed to know what new directions social forces were taking and how he could influence them. He made history; it was unnecessary for him to wait, as Bismarck said we must, while it was being made around him. He put himself into events before there was any organized intervention.

It is biographer Larry Hannant's view that Bethune became the great figure he did because despite his flaws of impatience and irritability, he was capable of changing, "and the change, especially in the final two years of his life, when he was in China, was beneficial.... His spirit of selflessness flourished."

The moral imperative born into Bethune as the son of a Presbyterian minister never really died in him. It was diluted with other beliefs, but the ethical standards and morality of Presbyterianism were always there in the way in which he looked at the world. "I know I'm always in a hurry," he once said, "but I come by this trait honestly. My father was a Presbyterian minister who joined the Moody and Sankey Evangelical movement. Their slogan was 'the world for Christ in one generation' and this is my slogan, whether people like it or not." Bethune did not mean the specific idea of making people Christians, but the power of revolutionary belief as a way to transform people, and transform them forever. Compassionate identification with suffering and helplessness was always his way. Starting in his adolescence with his work for Frontier College and his actions as a stretcher-bearer in the horror of the First World War, he showed himself to be someone who wanted to take care of his fellow human beings.

In the opinion of Hazen Sise, his friend and colleague in Spain, Bethune would have been enormously grateful for his sanctification in China, but he would also have found it hilarious. Not because he doubted the Chinese and their sincerity, but because to think of himself as a hero or a saint was not in his character. Those who knew Bethune, like Sise, and had seen him under the most difficult conditions in Spain, agree that he was a great man, but that he never once thought of himself as superhuman. Sise says, "Bethune [was]

capable of so happy and spontaneous an outpouring of energy … even the morose would brighten up when he entered
the room…. He had another important trait … the ability
to remorselessly base his beliefs on reality rather than preju-
dice or self-interest … to live in the light of his beliefs."

Everyone approaches Bethune with his or her own particular set of baggage. Ted Allan, the writer who was close to
Bethune during the months that he was in Spain, acting
often as his spokesperson, felt he was some kind of spiritual
son to Bethune, and for the rest of his life Allan considered
himself the guardian and keeper of the flame. No document
in Bethune's archives could be consulted without his permis-
sion. For years he kept people from consulting them at all.
No one ever found out by what right Ted Allan thought he
could do this, as there is no will in which Allan is named as
Bethune's executor. With his book *The Scalpel, the Sword*,
which he co-authored with Sydney Gordon, a fellow
Communist, he put forth his vision of Bethune as a hero,
basing his work largely on a Chinese novel of the late 1940s
by Zhou Erfu. His touching attempts to draw himself as
Norman Bethune's sole executor and custodian must be
viewed as the actions of someone who felt that Communism
would never die as long as he could keep the ashes of one of
its ranking saints in his own personal reliquary. This idea that

somehow the myth could be owned and that one could be the gatekeeper to a personality is belied by Norman Bethune's own actions during his lifetime. He once had a bookplate made that stated, "This book belongs to Norman Bethune and all his friends." He thought of his life the same way: it belonged to all his friends. He was part of them. There is no indication that Bethune, with all his dynamism and focus and determination, wasn't a good friend and a faithful ally.

Bethune became a Communist in 1935, which tarnished him in many eyes. Certainly it accounts for the fact that he was neglected, nearly forgotten, in his own country before 1971 and the beginning of Canada's diplomatic relationship with the People's Republic of China. It was almost as though he was being blamed for having been raised to heroic stature by the Chinese. Surprisingly, this anti-Bethune feeling continues in some circles. The fact that a Canadian could be venerated abroad is difficult for some to accept, and the "Who do you think you are anyway?" attitude toward great, but necessarily flawed, people has operated on a particularly high level where Bethune is concerned. But there's nothing in either Bethune's letters or the accounts of his actions by the Chinese that indicates he was out for self-glorification.

After Canada and China exchanged ambassadors in 1971, years of television documentaries, films, and books on

Bethune poured out of Canada, as they had been coming out of China for decades. In 2004, the Chinese made yet another thirteen-hour television series about him. In his own lifetime, Bethune had already caught the imagination of many. First among them was a rising group of Montreal intellectuals in the 1930s who would go on to define much of modern Canada. Montreal celebrates him with a large statue in a prominent square and is proud of the eight years he spent there. Many people believe that he is a Montrealer. Toronto and Ontario, apart from his little birthplace of Gravenhurst, pay him no mind. There is a Bethune Roundtable on International Surgery, which states that it is named in honour of Norman Bethune, Canada's best-known international surgeon. York University in Toronto has a Bethune College. That's it. So where is the statue or the lecture hall or the square to acknowledge that Bethune graduated in medicine from the University of Toronto? Or that for a number of winters he went to work in the lumber camps for Frontier College, or that he lived at 19 Harbord Street in Toronto, or that in 1937 he spoke to three thousand people at Massey Hall? None of this is marked or celebrated. Perhaps people in Toronto felt the way the Historic Sites and Monuments Board of Canada felt in October 1971 when it assessed Bethune's medical career in the context of a history of medicine in Canada: it found that "Dr. Bethune's career was not of national historic importance."

But elsewhere he made a deeper impression. No other Canadian has inspired as great a novel as Hugh MacLennan's *The Watch That Ends the Night*, published in 1959. Its hero, Dr. Jerome Martell, is clearly modelled on Norman Bethune, whom MacLennan knew well in Montreal in those early years but whom he never acknowledged as the basis of the character.

The novel's plot is simple. The protagonist, George Stewart, is married to Catherine, who has a rheumatic heart condition (as MacLennan's own wife did). Catherine was previously married to Martell, who, after a brilliant medical career in Montreal in the 1930s, went to the Spanish Civil War and later disappeared into the French underground during the Nazi occupation in the Second World War. They were all told that he had been caught as a spy and taken to Buchenwald, where he was hung on a meat hook and died.

The book begins with the surprise return of Martell, who has survived the horrors of fascism in Europe. The story unspools from there. Martell was born to an illiterate logging-camp cook in New Brunswick who was murdered when Martell was ten years old. He escaped down the river in a tiny canoe, was found wandering at a train station, and was then adopted by a kindly clergyman and his wife. The most fascinating part of the novel is this story of Jerome Martell coming out of the wilderness, the inspiration for which may have come from MacLennan hearing Bethune speak about his adolescence in the logging camps and wilderness of northern Ontario. Certainly it is as far from MacLennan's own experience as anything could be.

This drama is woven into a background of George's despair about how the beliefs and passions of the 1930s had come to nothing in the 1950s. The return of Martell is like the return of an old dream, an old passion, a commitment to beliefs and action that are no longer possible in the grey Canada of the 1950s. George admired and envied the huge figure that Martell cut among his contemporaries.

> Jerome ... could never belong to any particular group of human beings; he belonged to humanity itself. This he never seemed to know. He had less ordinary social sense than anyone I ever knew, and if he met the King of England he would have been interested in him solely as a human being and if the King bored him he would have been quite capable of changing the subject or walking away to talk to somebody else. He was utterly without a

sense of class distinction and the subtle layers of these distinctions in Montreal entirely escaped his notice. I'm sure he was snubbed dozens of times; I'm equally sure he never noticed it.

Martell says to George:

> You must learn to build a shell around yourself like a snail and every now and then you must creep inside of it.... The shell is death. You must crawl inside of death and die yourself.... When things become intolerable—you must die within yourself. Your soul is making your body revolt against what you think you have to bear. You can only live again by facing death. Then you outface it. You must say to yourself and mean it when you say it, 'What difference does it make if I die? What difference does it make if I am disgraced? What difference does it make if everything we've done means nothing?' You must say these things and believe them. Then you will live.

What does this mean? Martell is perfectly lucid about the implication.

I am not a revolutionary ... it gets damn lonely bucking the current all the time.... It's always seemed to me an incredible privilege to belong to civilization.... Unless fascism is stopped in Spain ... there will be a war we'll probably lose. I know that's what fascism is. It's not political at all, it's simply the organization of every murderous impulse in a human being.

Novelist Robertson Davies, who also never acknowledged that Bethune was the prototype for Martell, says in his 1959 review of *The Watch That Ends the Night*:

[Here] the Canadian novel takes a great stride forward.... Martell may appear ... as a truly great man, or merely as a man who mistakes his own abundant energy for thought, like all such people, he is a two-edged sword, bringing fulfillment to some and ruin to others.... But a literature has no hope of maturity until its writers embark on precisely this task of capturing the subtleties of human feeling and conduct, and revealing them as manifested in their countrymen.

It seems that Bethune's life made it possible for MacLennan to write one of the greatest Canadian novels. MacLennan said he had wanted to "write a book which would not depend on character-in-action, but on spirit-in-action." Bethune was part of the shedding of the cloak of colonialism in Canada. "No writer can jump the gap until his society has grown across it like a bridge; until the spirit of his society has merged with that of the world." Bethune embodied that spirit.

Norman Bethune is compelling because he reached through the dark for all the things that really mattered in the light. In China, he became another creature, living in a torn land, a creature not of the Chinese but also no longer of us either. His character found its transformation. MacLennan understood the meaning of Bethune's life: "Embracing the unknown, moving on through possibilities to action and taking for granted that everything that happens to you can be accepted and absorbed."

CHAPTER TWO

Everything Bathed in Timelessness

Standing at the front door of Norman Bethune's childhood house in Gravenhurst, you imagine that the spot where he was born looked then as it does now—neat and prim with its freshly painted clapboard siding. You are in a place of contradictions: small-town Ontario on Lake Muskoka, the largest of the three Muskoka lakes, the others being Lake Joseph and Lake Rosseau. These lakes 180 kilometres north of Toronto have been open to the depredations of civilization since the mid-nineteenth century.

Discerning rich Americans came from Pittsburgh, Philadelphia, and New York to settle for the summer. These legendary families, many of whose palatial cottages are still maintained, brought with them their servants and furnished their houses with idiosyncratic twig furniture, monogrammed linen, porcelain, and sterling silver. Their custom helped to establish the in-board motorboat factories in the area. These elegant craft cut the waters of the Muskoka lakes like honed knives, providing transport and also pleasure trips to islands that were carefully preserved in their natural state as destinations for picnics on warm summer days.

Bethune lived his first few years in this southernmost part of the Canadian Shield. The Shield breaks through some forty kilometres before you actually get to Muskoka, and suddenly you are confronted with a dramatic change in landscape, the rocks sparkling pink, white, and black. The granite is more than half feldspar, which has a crystalline quality; a third is white or transparent quartz; and the rest is mica or hornblende. You cannot see these rocks without wondering how they were formed, in what turbulence they were tossed in molten form until they oozed into place and hardened in the sinuous shapes found along the shores with water lapping implacably at their edges. In some places, the rocks look like marble cake, the elements kept deliberately separate, yet folded over one another to make a petrified batter.

The Canadian Shield is the single greatest factor in creating the original wealth of our country. In this geological formation we have found gold, silver, nickel, copper, platinum, uranium, lead, zinc, and cobalt. The whole concept and exploitation of Canada as a nation of commodities is our gift from the Shield.

The logging practised since the mid-nineteenth century did not spare Muskoka: no first-growth forest survives. People now older than eighty who cottaged in this area remember that the trees were once very small and that the remains of logging—deadheads in the water, stumps on the shores—were common.

It would be difficult to explain this history of geological and industrial violence to the thousands of Chinese visitors who stream through Bethune's house every year. They must simply accept that the birthplace of their greatest foreign hero does not have the same significance for Canadians as it does for them.

When Bethune was born in 1890, his father had the charge of the local Presbyterian church and Canada was just more than twenty years old as a federation. Gravenhurst was nicknamed Sawdust City, with its men living on their own in camps through the winter.

The whole area is dotted with the sad remains of settlers' roads through swamps and rock-strewn areas that could never support agriculture, even after painful clearing. Bethune, with his indomitable spirit, sprang right out of this granite, this hard land that made farming heartbreaking, virtually impossible.

Bethune lived out his childhood in towns like this as his peripatetic father and the calling of the Church moved the family from place to place all around the Shield—Beaverton, Owen Sound, Aylmer, Blind River—where the lakes and land in poet Douglas LePan's words were "vivid blue … [and] trees green … [with] everything bathed in timelessness."

The lakes were wonderfully swimmable in the summer and could be cleared for skating in the winter. Bethune would have seen and been familiar with black bears, moose, deer, beavers, otters, wolves, lynxes, foxes, and the now-rare Massassauga rattlesnake. Living on the thin crust of earth over granite, growing up in this fragile geography and climate—blazing hot summers, frigid winters, and exquisitely coloured autumns—would influence the way he looked at things all his life.

Pictured on sports teams at Owen Sound Collegiate, from which Bethune graduated before going to the University of Toronto, is a hearty adolescent of no particular distinction—a square head, firm mouth, and bright eyes. It is hard to see in that solid specimen the quasi-mystical figure he later became.

In Bethune's youth, Owen Sound was a big port on the south shore of Georgian Bay, an enormous arm of Lake Huron. Contemporary photos show considerable shipping activity and huge docks, which created wealth not only for that city but also for its neighbours on the Bay—Penetanguishene, Collingwood, and Midland. The area was filled with factories that used sub-products of the forest industry, such as hemlock bark, which was ground into the tanbark used for processing leather. Owners of factories and shipping companies lived in handsome houses of brick or beautifully hewn clapboard. Photographs show us men in frock coats and women in fashionable corsets playing croquet on the lawns in front of their homes. Interestingly enough, in the mid-nineteenth century Owen Sound was also a terminal of the Underground Railway, which brought escaped slaves from the United States to freedom in Canada. When Bethune lived there, 10 percent of the population of Owen Sound was black.

He was the son of Malcolm Bethune and Elizabeth Ann Goodwin. After graduating from Upper Canada College, Malcolm had travelled around the world until he ended up in Hawaii, where he met Elizabeth, who was an Evangelical missionary. Presumably at her urging, example, or insistence, he became a Presbyterian clergyman.

The Bethune family has its roots in Normandy. The town of Bethune is just kilometres from Vimy Ridge, the site of the Canadians' great victory in April 1917. Bethunes have been recorded in that part of France since the eleventh century. They believed that they dated back to William the Conqueror, that their name was originally Betoun. In 1773 a John Bethune emigrated to North Carolina from the Isle of Skye. He was a descendant of generations of doctors and, as the documents put it, "men of peace." John Bethune's father was wounded at Culloden in 1745, but we don't know which side he fought for—Bonnie Prince Charlie or the English government. Caught up in the American Revolution, John Bethune became chaplain to the Royal Highland Emigrants and was taken prisoner by the revolutionary forces in 1776. He spent two years in prison, and upon being freed he fled to Canada, thereby qualifying as a Loyalist. He founded the first Presbyterian congregation in Montreal. Later he became the first Presbyterian minister in Ontario and married a rich heiress, the daughter of a Swiss fur trader. They had a son, Angus, who became a merchant. He had a brilliant career and eventually became director of the Bank of Upper Canada. When he was younger, Angus led an adventurous life, crossing the Pacific and Atlantic, living among the Aboriginals and marrying a young Aboriginal woman. Later, he married Louisa McKenzie. The second of their six children was Norman Bethune, born in 1822 at Moose Factory, Ontario. In 1840 Norman was enrolled at

Toronto's Upper Canada College, and in 1845, he attended King's College Medical School. At the end of the 1850s, Norman went (as his grandson did after him) to Edinburgh, where he qualified as a surgeon and was made a fellow of the Royal College of Physicians of Edinburgh. He had studied in Strasbourg and later witnessed the battle of Solferino, which was part of the Italian Risorgimento, the political and social movement than unified Italy (not to be confused with the Napoleonic battle of Solferino, but just as terrible and bloody). Norman was noted as an excellent surgeon and became acquainted with Henry Dunant, who had just conceived the idea of the Red Cross. He then practised in Brescia, in northern Italy. Dr. Bethune was described by Dr. Carlo Cotta, the Royal Health Inspector of the region of Lombardy, in July 1859, as "a professor of anatomy from Toronto who rushed ... to dedicate himself to doctoring the wounded and who carried out brilliant operations of skilful surgery at San Girolamo Hospital (and who didn't want to hear talk of any thanks). He quietly took his leave without goodbye as soon as he saw that the need for his contribution had become less.... This generous foreign volunteer [was] spurred to help us out of a deep sense of human generosity."

Norman Bethune had clearly been caught up in the era's atmosphere of international humanitarianism. Back in

Canada, he became a consultant professor to the Toronto Medical Hospital. His son, Malcolm, Bethune's father, apparently took good care of him throughout the rest of his life, which was marred disastrously by alcoholism. Norman had artistic interests and created sketches that showed some talent and technique, all skills inherited by his grandson and namesake.

In our secular age, the fact that someone was the son of a Presbyterian minister may seem to be a mere detail—such as hair colour, or height, or an aptitude for a particular sport. But, in fact, religion was an overwhelming consideration in the Canada into which Norman Bethune was born. His formative years were governed by the rhythms of the Bible, by tithing to support missionaries, and by observing the Sabbath as a day of rest. Being a Presbyterian in the 1890s involved going to church at least twice on Sunday and reading the Bible in the afternoon at home during the week. Grace would have been said at the beginning of every meal, to thank God for his blessings and ask succour for those not so fortunate. The clergyman's family had to set an example for the community of a life lived by religious principles— doing good to your fellow man, living by the Ten Commandments, and generally eschewing the devil and all his works. For Norman Bethune and his younger siblings,

Malcolm and Janet, this was a considerable and unques-
tioned part of their lives.

The Westminster Confession of the Church of Scotland,
which in 1647 laid out the doctrines of the Presbyterian
Church, is a stern and uncompromising document. It makes
clear the two important tenets for which the church was
known—predestination and the reality of hell. In Chapter 3
it is stated: "By the decree of God, for the manifestation of
His glory, some men and angels are predestinated unto everlasting life; and others foreordained to everlasting death."
The scriptural justification for this is in Matthew 25:41:
"Then shall He say also unto them on the left hand, Depart
from me, ye cursed, into everlasting fire, prepared for the
Devil and his angels." Next: "These angels and men, thus
predestinated, and foreordained, are particularly and
unchangeably designed, and their numbers so certain and
definite, that it cannot be either increased or diminished."

One can only imagine the effect that this doctrine would
have had on a young child, especially one with an argumen-
tative and self-confident personality. Bethune referred frequently to predestination. But he didn't appear to believe he
was one of God's chosen or that salvation was his destiny.
Quite the opposite: he challenged the idea that he could be
predestined for good or evil. Instead he would live his life

demanding everything of it that it had to give, salvation or no salvation. But the concept haunted him, he mentioned it frequently, and in the myth built out of his death there is that shadow of predestination.

The years of Bethune's childhood were a time of enormous missionary fervour. In the 1896–97 Annual Report of the Canadian Methodist Church Missionary Society, Christians are exhorted as follows: "Enlighten China and you have illuminated the Eastern world. Move China and you move the world. Save China and the problem of the world's salvation is solved." All his life Bethune would have heard of China and the souls to be harvested there.

It's hard for us to imagine now, in our secular society, what the passions were at the time. How deeply, for instance, the Grey Nuns and the Oblates of Quebec, the Methodists and Presbyterians of Nova Scotia and Ontario, and the Anglicans of British Columbia and Toronto felt their calling as missionaries to save an entire continent. They had been challenged to become the "church militants." Popular American evangelist Dwight Moody, who influenced Norman Bethune's parents and was the Billy Graham of his day, came to Toronto in 1885 preaching his version of "sanctified common sense" to twenty thousand people—calculated to be half the adult population of the city. Young people in the city's parishes were told that they were personally, individually, responsible for the salvation of the world and that they must go and achieve it. They were to be satisfied with nothing less than the evangelization of the world in one generation, and China was their goal. Fifty years later, China also became Bethune's goal, but for a different reason.

In 1888, a torchlight parade of one thousand young people escorted the first large Canadian party of missionaries bound for China to Toronto's train station. In the early twentieth century, within the two square miles bounded by Toronto's College, Bathurst, Sherbourne, and Bloor streets, there were twenty-five missionary-sending institutions and thirty churches that had made saving China a major purpose for their alms. Never again would so large a party of Christian soldiers go onward, marching as to war. Some say that by doing what he did, ironically Bethune became Canada's greatest missionary, because his help to the Chinese in two critical years was an example of selflessness and determination to put others first.

As the child of a Presbyterian minister, Bethune absorbed the climate of excitement surrounding the church at the turn of the century, where much liberal theology was emerging, particularly in the sermons of Reverend J.S. MacDonnell, the minister at St. Andrew's Presbyterian Church at King and Simcoe streets in Toronto. In 1875, MacDonnell had declared from the pulpit his doubts about "the doctrine of eternal punishment" and whether there was a real hell with flames.

MacDonnell contrasted strongly the message of Divine Love in the New Testament with the stony doctrine of double predestination (salvation or damnation) in the Westminster Confession. In short, MacDonnell was urging a return to the New Testament and Christ's words, which, he said, were more valid than doctrinal structure. MacDonnell's stand enabled many Presbyterians to rethink their own beliefs and ultimately led a number to join the group that in 1926, with Methodists and Congregationalists, became the United Church of Canada. Bethune's father was one of them. Despite sensational newspaper coverage and public denunciation, MacDonnell emerged from a heresy trial unscathed, establishing St. Andrew's as a centre of liberal theology and tolerance.

MacDonnell was dealing with another kind of hell in downtown Toronto. It was a sordid city, filled with exploited child workers, prostitution, and public drunkenness. Many of its inhabitants lived in tenements and tarpaper lean-tos, and every second commercial establishment seemed to be a bar or gin shop. Children went without shoes, and illiteracy was the norm. The reeking slums, with their eighteen thousand outdoor privies and mud and horse manure in the streets, were very real to the parishioners of all churches and undoubtedly were a great influence on their attempts to better the world they saw immediately around them. In the early twentieth century, when Norman Bethune was studying at the University of Toronto, these conditions still prevailed. He lived on Harbord Street, close to Kensington Market, an area that was filling with needy immigrants from Eastern Europe, including many Jews. But the house on Harbord was also just two blocks from Knox College, the University of Toronto's Presbyterian theological college then located on Spadina Crescent.

He must have thought about it a lot: What was he destined to do? Was he one of the elect? Even if he wasn't, the conditions were right to inspire him to do the best he could for others. It must have been a shock for a small-town boy like him to find himself in a city like Toronto, which was teeming with filth and disorder—he who had known the pristine water of Georgian Bay and the smell of pine. Not everyone could be part of what he had experienced, and it must have struck him as being unjust.

It is hard to know what Bethune's father made of the evolution of the church around him in those years. Bethune's few words about his father were never loving and usually condemning; at one point we are told by Bethune's ex-wife (not a totally reliable source) that Malcolm once pushed young Norman's face into the dirt and made him eat it in order to teach him humility.

Malcolm's example did not lead Bethune to commit his life to the kind of God his father believed in; it led him to another reality, another manifestation of good that he thought attainable in this world. The divisions in the Presbyterian Church he grew up with, and the divisions in his own family, prepared him for dissent, argument, and a sense that not everything was what it seemed.

There are many indications from Bethune in later life that he did not get on with his parents. His provocative self-confidence probably drove them nearly insane. One can only imagine the kind of heated discussions that took place between Bethune and a mother who, as an Evangelical, was obedient only to an invisible power, and a father who could not come to terms with his proud, arrogant son. Bethune's biographer Roderick Stewart tells us that Bethune was particularly contemptuous of his father for becoming enraged with him and then later coming to his son to beg forgiveness. It's hard to know what irritated the young Bethune more—being the object of a rage he despised or being the recipient of an apology he had not sought. The clash between the religious parents terrified by God and His mysterious will and the son whose character was choleric, individualistic, and sensitized by burning curiosity was inevitable. All the attributes that were going to make him the person he needed to become would have irritated and exasperated both his parents.

CHAPTER THREE

Reach Out and Take the Hand of the Toiler

Perhaps Bethune wanted to be a doctor because the first Norman Bethune had lived such an adventurous and exciting life on the battlefields in Europe. Perhaps Bethune realized that the humanitarian in his grandfather was part of what his own fate should be.

Right after high school, Bethune, who loved sports and wasn't particularly interested in things intellectual, went to work for a year in a lumber camp in Algoma, in northern Ontario. It consolidated his love for the woods. Nature and the Canadian Shield represented to him not simply pleasant holidays, they were a fact of his life; he was born close to the wilderness and he could contend with it. A logging camp was nevertheless a tough place to live. He was a minister's son, and for the first time he learned what it was like to live day to day working in very dangerous circumstances—logging in deep snow, dragging logs to the river where they would form a huge boom, sawing the trees into lengths, rolling on logs, and giving orders in difficult situations to teams of immigrant men who did not speak English.

He took various jobs, interrupting his education for up to a year at a time. He taught for six months in a one-room school in the village of Edgeley, near Toronto, and earned $269, which was quite a sum of money. This, together with the logging money, financed his medical studies at the University of Toronto.

Then he went to work in camps with a specific purpose: Bethune taught his fellow workers reading and writing in the evenings as a member of Frontier College. Alfred Fitzpatrick had founded the movement in 1899. He saw the desperate need for education in the mining and lumber camps that were producing the commodities that were making Ontario rich. Up to 70 percent of all the workers in frontier lumber camps were illiterate. And 75 percent were unable to calculate whether they had been fairly paid. Because of their remoteness from towns or cities, the workers could not improve themselves. There was nothing to read, no alphabet to be seen anywhere in the camp at all except in the wrappings of patent medicine bottles. In any case, the meagre light they were provided with in their sleeping shacks would have hardly permitted reading. The harsh conditions meant that frontier labour was very difficult to come by, and so the number of immigrants was increased dramatically to fill the need for workers, growing from twenty-one thousand in 1897 to more than four hundred thousand in 1911. Between 1890 and 1910, the time of Bethune's youth, the population of Canada as a whole grew by 32 percent, mostly through immigration. Fitzpatrick's desire to better the lot of frontier workers was inspired by his outrage at their appalling living conditions and their exploitation, to all intents and purposes, as beasts of burden. He believed that learning was possible in such deprived circumstances. Through Frontier College, he worked for improved living conditions, social welfare, and education, and he found a way to deliver that message through the labourer-teacher. Norman Bethune was one of the earliest.

"To many of the foreigners, the labourer-teacher is a new type of Canadian—clean in life and lip, yet straightforward and doing a man's work alongside them," wrote Fitzpatrick. "He stands for staunch Canadianism and British institutions, and teaches by example and daily wear and tear. He is measured by his worth, not his theory. Quietly and unassumedly, he is a molder of Canadianism." He looked for frontier teachers among university students and therefore shifted the association's emphasis from winter to summer work to adapt to students' schedules. Working during the day with the men and teaching at night became a natural pattern, and the teachers were regarded as co-workers on the same level as their students. The labourer-teachers were paid by the lumber camp for their daytime manual work, and for their teaching they got a small honorarium. Fitzpatrick described their work thus: "They [have donned the rough dress] of the frontiersman and engaged in every kind of labour known to the frontier. They may be seen shooting the rapids of a mountain river … driving mules … working on a bridge or trestle, cooking, building dumps, timber sawing, 'chickadeeing,' (picking obstructions off the main trail), 'falling [trees],' acting as 'beavers' (cutting trails), and engaging in a score of other occupations."

Many of the labourer-teachers were from cities and totally unused to manual labour. They were given the toughest jobs to test their abilities. Bethune thrived on this challenge. To Fitzpatrick he wrote, "Please send instruction books in Polish and French as soon as possible. There are about a dozen men in camp who cannot speak English. It is extremely desirable that they know something at least about the language when they leave in the spring. These books are small and plain-lettered with simple sentences. Until they come, very little can be done along this line."

He worked as an axeman and with engines that pulled logs uphill. He also played a squeaky phonograph for his co-workers and, being a medical student, was able to help with minor injuries and first aid.

There were overtly nationalistic messages in everything that the instructors did. The much-used *Handbook for New Canadians* was designed to teach English to adults by presenting English vocabulary useful in situations in which an immigrant would confront Canadian life, but it was also designed to inspire loyalty to the immigrants' new country and overcome any undesirable influences they might have brought from their European backgrounds by suggesting behaviour more suitable to life in Canada. They were lectured on current events, on government, on mechanics, and on land settlement. Church groups and the YMCA helped to send books and magazines.

Bethune wrote to Fitzpatrick from Pineage Lake, Ontario: "[Everything is] progressing favourably. [I] spent time laying in a supply of wood, plastering and arranging the comforts of an effete civilization in conformity with strict mission-style furnishings.... I have commenced work on the road." He complained of "blisters and fully developed symptoms of a kink in my vertebral column," but stated that

I enjoy [the work] now and I'm sure I am going to like it immensely later on. Would you please be so kind as to send me the following?

A small English dictionary

A couple of pads of this paper

Some copies of the *Illustrated London News, Black and White*, etc.

A few Bibles …

A dozen paper-covered Alexander's Hymn book, used by the revivalist committee—where is my wandering boy tonight, and all those kinds of songs …

Note—this is not a joke.

Regarding *The Saturday Evening Post*, he wrote:

It is read with a great deal of interest.… Will you subscribe to it in my name, for I will gladly pay the subscription to have it in the camp.

I'm sending you a list of my records on a separate sheet. Would be very grateful if a couple of dozen more records could be sent. Some of the records here are practically useless from rough usage … providing a combination of shrills and shrieks not included in the original definition of harmony by the great Wagner.

Fitzpatrick noted that labourer-teachers also acted as "fathers, confessors, chums and confidants." They wrote letters, prepared mail orders, and helped to organize recreational activities such as sports, musical events, and singalongs. All of this helped immigrant workers learn about what life was really like in Canada. The values that Fitzpatrick believed in and which he hoped labourer-teachers such as Bethune would convey were mainstream Anglo-Saxon Protestant characteristics, including cleanliness, honesty, and chivalry, which they had to teach by example. The message Bethune helped to convey through the *Handbook* required that a good citizen "loves God; loves the Empire; loves Canada; loves his own family; protects women and children; works hard; does his work well; helps his neighbours; is truthful; is just; is honest; is brave; keeps his promise; his body is clean; he is in every inch a man." The majority of labourer-teachers were Protestant, although there were some Catholics and Jews. Initially they were expected to have to lead some form of religious service, but that gradually became less important; Fitzpatrick believed it was more important that the labourer-teacher be ethical than that he be attached to any particular church.

Fitzpatrick felt that by choosing university students he was taking advantage of the position of privilege they enjoyed; he also wrote that "it is because the university graduate is in the position to obtain the interest and aid of the capitalist that he above all others must reach out and take the hand of the toiler."

In the lumber camps Bethune developed a sense of camaraderie and brotherhood with a world of men who were completely foreign to him. It awakened him to the dreadful conditions and awesome challenges of the working class. He learned to believe in the betterment of his fellow man, to be willing to sacrifice his own comfort to help others, and to teach and communicate with anyone across any cultural or language barrier.

Bethune returned to university in 1912 to continue his medical studies, undeterred by mediocre marks.

At the outbreak of the First World War, in August 1914, the young men of Canada rushed to join up, to go overseas and defend civilization against the German Kaiser. By September 25, six weeks after war was declared, Norman Bethune, medical student at the University of Toronto, residing at 19 Harbord Street in Toronto, had joined the

No. 2 Field Ambulance of the Canadian Expeditionary Force at Valcartier. Described in official documents as a Presbyterian with blue eyes, brown hair, and a height of 5'10", bearing the marks of two vaccinations on his left arm and a scar on his inner left thigh, he was certified to be "fit" to proceed overseas from Quebec on the SS *Cassandra* (perhaps not the most promising name for a ship carrying soldiers to battle).

Bethune chose to serve as a stretcher-bearer. On arriving in Europe he joined the First Canadian Division near the town of Ypres, in Belgium. At the time, the Canadians were fighting beside the French, Belgian, and British armies, living in the newly dug trenches that would over the next four years become a hell on earth. The trenches had fiendish twists and turns to accommodate the posts for guns. From October on they were filled with water, mud, and rats. To become a stretcher-bearer was a logical choice for Bethune: he had medical training and he was used to physical labour. His job was to carry wounded soldiers, bleeding or writhing in agony, from the battlefield back into the trenches, where they could be treated in medical stations and then moved farther away to larger facilities. It was an experience that probably marked Bethune forever. A stretcher-bearer was exposed to all the dangers of a combatant but was devoted only to saving the lives of others. This was a deliberate choice on Bethune's part, suggesting that while not a pacifist, he wished to save lives rather than be called upon to bayonet somebody his own age.

As a private, he had to obey others' orders, and for six months during the winter of 1914–15 he did his job. At the second battle of Ypres, on April 29, 1915, he suffered a wound from shrapnel or gunshot in the leg, with the projectile going right through his shin bone and exiting through the back of his leg. He was given anti-tetanus immediately. Then he himself was carried on a stretcher to an aid station, then to a hospital, after which he was put on a train and shipped out to England. The wound was serious enough that he spent six months recuperating in Britain before being sent home. He was fortunate not to lose his leg. His papers were stamped at the discharge depot in Quebec on November 2, 1915, and he was released from service "in consequence of being medically unfit." It was also noted that his military character was "exemplary."

What can we surmise about Norman Bethune's experience in the First World War? For one thing, he saw firsthand how difficult it was to get the wounded quickly to a first-aid station and from there to more sophisticated facilities. He must have carried many soldiers who bled to death with no hope of receiving a transfusion in time. Saving lives on the front line in Spain and China was in many ways a continuation of this first troubling and dangerous confrontation with war. It seems that nothing that happened to him was ever meaningless: every experience gave significance and vitality to decisions that he would later make. Many people describe him as swift to action, but he was not purely impulsive. Once he decided what he thought could be done, he simply moved to doing it without wasting time.

Having left medical school on the outbreak of war, just before his third year was to begin, Bethune returned to do an accelerated program, which meant that he graduated in 1916 (at the same time as Frederick Banting, who would go on to be a co-discoverer of insulin). He then decided to return to the conflict that was still consuming his own country and Europe; in 1917 he became a lieutenant surgeon and was stationed aboard HMS *Pegasus* with the Royal Navy, doing active duty in the North Sea. He served until early in 1919, after the war had ended. He also managed to spend part of a year as a medical officer in the new Canadian Air Force, doing research on the causes of blackouts in pilots. So in four years Bethune served in the army, the navy, and the air force. It seems to show a great desire to be part of the action, to know where the puck is going, as Wayne Gretzky says, and to skate toward it.

Bethune's eagerness to experience all aspects of the war is an indication of a certain kind of hyperactivity, which is probably not entirely about patriotism or altruism but an avid curiosity and desire to try everything. There was really no need for him to go back and join the Royal Navy—he had received an honourable discharge. It was as if he felt the need to prove something to himself. It was a quality that made him particularly irritating to a number of his contemporaries, but being the kind of self-actualizing person he was, he didn't give a damn what they thought of him. "My father was an evangelist," he told a friend, "and I come of a race of men violent and unstable, of passionate convictions and wrongheadedness, intolerant, yet with it all a vision of truth and a drive to carry them on to it even though it leads, as it has done in my family, to their own destruction—as it did my father." The idea of predestination lurks here: if that meant being in three branches of the armed forces in a single war, so be it.

CHAPTER FOUR

Fear Is the Great Destroyer of Happiness

In 1920 Bethune worked at the Great Ormond Street Hospital for Children and the West London Hospital in England. He enjoyed living in London, haunting the art galleries and buying sketches, drawings, and paintings, indulging a taste he had developed for tailor-made suits. Although he did not have the income to match his tastes, he seems to have had a wonderful time anyway. In London, he met a young Scottish woman named Frances Penney. Photos show her to be serious, with a fashionable bob haircut. Her family was respectable, conventional, and well-off. Their courtship lasted for three years, and in 1923 they were married at the London Registry Office. They proceeded to have a carefree six months in Europe, spending almost all of a legacy she had received from her uncle. We don't know much about Frances Penney except what can be gleaned from the surviving letters between her and Bethune. She had a privileged upbringing and had gone to a finishing school to prepare her for an appropriate marriage. She was waiting for her Prince Charming when this dashing doctor arrived from the wilds of Canada, obtained his fellowship in the Royal College of Surgeons of Edinburgh, and swept her off her feet.

There is nothing in their correspondence that indicates they were suited to each other; indeed there is much evidence that things were never right between them. Within ten years they had married and divorced each other twice, with Bethune maintaining all along in an irritating, jocular way that she would always be his wife and he was only loaning her out to others. Delving deeper, it becomes clear that he was bitterly disappointed at the difficulties they encountered and never expected to find himself in such a position. It's a curious anomaly in Bethune's life that he chose a wife who did not seem to have anything interesting about her and who was not even vaguely interested in what he was ready to die for. They did not have any children, and reading some of Bethune's letters to her, you wonder whether they ever really had sex.

> I regret—it is a constant pain in my heart, that I have harmed you. I did not intend to harm you.
>
> I was as ill-educated sexually as you—never forget that.

If I knew how to recompense you I would do
so....

My path is set on a strange road, but as long as
I feel it's a good road I will go down it. And you
must go down yours.

When I said I no longer have respect for you—
who I once respected—I meant, to me, your life
was devoid of dignity. But my dignity and your
dignity perhaps do not agree.

Mine is uncompromised; hatred of evil and stupidity, personal uncontamination and uncontact;
aloneness. That is all I meant. I see now once
more, I have made the mistake to suggest to you a
course of action. Forgive me. Beth

After they were divorced the first time in 1927 and she
had returned to Scotland to her family, he wrote to her
about his progress at the Royal Victoria Hospital in
Montreal, where he was initially very happy.

I can scarcely tell you, my darling Frances, how
glad for your sake this fellowship has turned up
[his salary enabled him to pay her alimony]. That
happiness of yours, is, to me, the most desired

thing in the world. If it were not for my doubts I would say it once—'come here. Marry me. Why should we be separate who love each other.'

I can be happy with you—but you, not with me.

I was thinking that if you came here this winter we could meet just as friends, living apart. In any case, whether you marry me or not, that is, I am sure, *our* only way.

Early the next year he wrote to her that he had spent Christmas with his family in Toronto.

Father and I had our usual hate together— especially heated as he is gambling on the stock market (made 500 dollars last year!) and I refused to drink his scotch and soda in the bathroom and had it in front of him. What hypocrites these professed religious are....

Work goes on as usual. I must look for a job in the States, I think, in the summer. I shall dislike leaving Montreal, but feel my life's ... a determined and predestined irregular one. So I accept it ... I am a different soul ... I wish you were here. I am glad you are relatively happy and well, at least more so than when relieved of my petulant irritability. God bless you, Beth.

About a month later he concluded a letter with these words:

I've often thought I'd like to surprise you by waiting at the corner of the street for you one morning as you walk down to the car. I'd just say, 'hullo—let's go for a walk.' And did we love each other in your dreams—were we in each other's arms again?

Later in 1929, they were married for the second time, but by 1931 they were separated again and discussing divorce. He wrote to her from a lecture trip in the United States.

Darling Frances,

Thank you for your two letters which were waiting for me on my return from Tucson.

I have noticed you think I forced you into marriage with RE [A.R.E. Coleman, one of Bethune's friends]. Believe me, I will never force you to do anything your heart is opposed to ever again. I love you and always will, however much it may hurt or wound me—and now all that is left for me to show you I love you is to help you to gain what you want. I can do that best by keeping you supplied with money, I think—for as someone has said, 'religion knows no peace comparable to that supplied by good clothes.' But I do think, my dear, the honourable thing is that if you are not going to marry RE is to tell me so—

1. I will not obtain a divorce.
2. Although it is not for me to dictate, nor will I now, do you think it is fair to keep him as a lover.

In the end, Bethune not only went to Frances and Coleman's wedding, but celebrated with the newlyweds afterwards.

When marrying Bethune, Frances probably didn't know what hit her. He had obviously been the first man in her life, and throughout their marriage, she desperately attempted to reconcile his efforts to control her with her own desire to be free of him. They annoyed each other intensely. Frances appeared to many to be "shallow, naïve, humourless and vindictive." But while she talked about Bethune endlessly, he never said a word about her in public. He later accused her of being "undignified," and asked her not to gossip about him. She was thrust alone into a world of which she knew nothing and for which she probably felt nothing but an ill-disguised contempt. Bethune returns again and again in his letters to the way they think differently and then goes off in cadenzas of poetic improvisation about the qualities of her soul. Finding herself caught up in Bethune's temperament and sense of destiny must have been confusing and even terrifying. Comments from many of their friends are not flattering to her, but, like many couples about whom friends ask "What on earth do they see in each other?" Frances and Bethune provide no answers. Bethune found Frances useful as a vessel for his ideas of what was good and decent about love. After all, he was brought up in a very puritan atmosphere by an extremely strict and, judging from photos, joyless mother. A painting of Frances by Bethune shows an idealized beauty, an attempt to demonstrate to himself, perhaps, that she was worth the emotional distress that he put himself through because of her. He writes:

> You are you and a self-contained, self-sufficient entity like a well buttressed little island that needs no connections with the external world to maintain its life and content.... But, darling, you're all

I've got in this world I care a rap about…. Our marriage has been wonderful for me. If I had to go over it again I would still want you for my side darling … keep a stiff upper lip—we, you and I, will beat them yet.

The emotions contending in these letters seem to establish a pattern in Bethune's relationship with his wife: he sympathizes with her, virtually throws himself at her feet, and then announces that he can be of no help whatsoever to her. He professes emotions, yet withdraws from the obligation of following through with what those emotions really mean.

In the myth-making about Bethune in the 1970s—the many movies and television programs—Frances and Bethune's relationship is portrayed as a kind of jazz-age Scott and Zelda Fitzgerald combination. It was far from that, and although they hurt nobody but each other, their marriage remained with Bethune as his unforgettable failure as a human being.

Bethune writes the following to Frances after she has married Coleman:

Truthfully and sincerely I believe I want nothing more from you. Not I as a man, physically, nor as a soul—spiritually. I believe we have had all the profitable commerce between us that is possible and nothing more is to be gained by prolongation of our relationship. It never at any time completely satisfied either of us—let us make no more attempts. I regret nothing of the past that has happened between us except one thing—my essential masculine stupidity on the non-recognition of reality and my fumbling attempts to change the fantasy into a fact ... don't try to please people....

Well, I will do my part—I will leave you alone....

That is the only way I can show I love you dearly. I can do nothing for you except leave you alone, entirely. We must die to each other.... Let us only remember it as a dream.

Goodbye my sweet Frances. I loved you once and to prove it, I will leave you now. Let us part. Goodbye. Beth.

PS—Show this letter to RE. I have written it as truthfully and sincerely as I am able. A truthful and sincere soul would accept it as such.

As is typical of Bethune in this relationship, this letter of farewell is in fact an effort to exert control. He's telling her that the relationship is over and he's telling her why it is over. He continues to tell her that he objectified her, while insisting that she cannot be changed. He lectures to his successor about how to triumph over his own emotions and then goes on to tell Frances how to improve her character by not trying to please people. The curious combination of domination and arrogance is breathtaking.

Whatever it was that Frances represented to him, he never really gave it up. In Jungian terms, she was his anima, and there was an element of self-destruction in his relationship with this anima that obviously suited him. Perhaps subconsciously it helped protect him against other women who were attracted to him. Dr. Aubrey Geddes, his flatmate between divorces, said:

> He had an extraordinary attraction to women. They loved to listen to him talk and they liked to follow him around. I don't think I ever knew anyone who attracted women to him more like a magnet than he did. One brilliant woman, I recall, and a very beautiful woman ... said, 'I saw him but once and he was the most aggressively male creature I had ever encountered.'

In 1924, the year after they were married the first time, the Bethunes made an exploratory trip to Canada to find out where Bethune might set up practice. The journey led them to Rouyn-Noranda in northern Quebec, which was being exploited as a gold mining centre, but Norman quickly realized he couldn't bring his British bride there. They went instead to Detroit, where he could be in private practice as well as work in a clinic for the poor (though Frances felt that Detroit was also beneath her). Detroit was a booming manufacturing centre, a good place for Bethune to repair his damaged fortunes and perhaps find neutral ground for their marriage, its being neither in Britain nor Canada. He began a steady practice, which gradually became lucrative, and he took on pro bono work in the seedier parts of town, where poverty, unemployment, and hopelessness had taken their toll. Wherever Bethune went, he took on work for people who couldn't pay. It may have been the custom of certain doctors before medicare to extend their services to the poor, but, as Bethune was soon saying in speeches to medical audiences, he was driven by his profound desire to take the profit out of medicine entirely.

In Detroit, he was popular and gregarious. As a member of the surgery department's outpatients' division at Harper Hospital, he was cross-appointed to the Detroit College of

Medicine and Surgery to teach prescription writing in the pharmacology department. He was making his way while infusing his teaching with a sense of humour. "This subject is a deadly bore but you must learn it and I will teach it to you," he said to the students. He was witty, anecdotal, beautifully dressed, and he seemed headed up the social ladder as a successful and well-paid surgeon. There was one drawback: Detroit itself. Frances despised the city and Americans even more than she despised Canadians.

After they'd been married nearly two years, Frances took a holiday alone in Nova Scotia and then went to California. She seemed to want to put continents between them. Bethune wrote gallant, contradictory letters assuring Frances that "I still love, worship and adore you my dearest. I am missing you frightfully but paradoxically wouldn't miss missing you for worlds. So please stay away a little longer." He continues: "At times this place overpowers even [me] and what it must do to your soul, my darling, I can only conjecture."

In fact, he had just been getting going financially—buying a car, acquiring a few paintings, and living in a more desirable area—when he received a terrifying medical diagnosis. In 1926, while Frances was away, Bethune, feeling exhausted and drained, submitted to a complete physical examination. He was diagnosed with tuberculosis in both lungs, at that time a virtual death sentence.

Research in the 1930s showed that most individuals with pulmonary tuberculosis were first exposed in adolescence. When they were infected from another source as adults, they would develop the full-blown disease. In Bethune's case, he would have been exposed to tuberculosis in his late teens when he worked for a year in northern Ontario before going to medical school, living in the close quarters of the logging cabins with poor immigrants. Then, as a doctor in Detroit, he would have come in contact with numerous patients with tuberculosis, which was very much in evidence in all North American cities, thriving in slum conditions and poverty. In Quebec alone, three thousand people died of tuberculosis in 1925. It was an epidemic: forty-eight thousand contracted tuberculosis annually in Canada, and two hundred out of every one hundred thousand people died of tuberculosis in Montreal and Toronto every year.

While on a waiting list for the renowned Trudeau Sanatorium at Saranac Lake, New York, Bethune returned to Gravenhurst, his birthplace, to stay for three months at the Calydor sanatorium. He thought it would be a brief interruption to his career. "I refuse to look at the dark side of things," he wrote to Frances. "[My practice in Detroit] is a gold mine if properly attended to, but thank God, I am out of that shaft.... I wept over one of the letters you wrote me—darling don't go home if you feel so bad about it but come to Toronto and at least we can be near each other." Very shortly afterwards, Frances returned to Scotland, as she had told him she intended to do, thereby initiating their separation.

After six months at the Trudeau Sanatorium, Bethune returned to Detroit to attempt to pick up some of his medical practice again, but less than three months later his tuberculosis flared alarmingly and he had to return to the sanatorium immediately. He began to lose hope and believed that he would die. He thought quite methodically about doing away with himself, and, according to biographer Roderick Stewart, told his friend John Barnwell that he had figured out he could inject himself with morphine and then swim into the lake, at which point the drug would take its effect and he would drown.

The Trudeau Sanatorium had a central building that was surrounded by attractive cottages in which groups of people were housed together. While there, Bethune decided to chart the course of his illness by painting a huge mural (now lost, but recorded in photos). Influenced by William Blake, it covered the walls of his cottage.

It is only the dull and unimaginative who can lie in a bed in a sanatorium for six months or a year and fail to rise a better and finer person. Life should be enriched and not impoverished by this retreat from the world.

The small cottage in which five of us lived ... was paneled in yellow pine ... there were four doors and three windows. [I made a] continuous coloured drawing five feet high and sixty feet long ... fitting in between the spaces in the roof and the wainscoting, the doors and windows. The title of the huge drawing was 'The TB's Progress, a Drama in One Act and Nine Painful Scenes'. Below the drawing were lines of poetry, describing the scenes.

In the mural Bethune progresses from a state of utter despair to a condition that he calls "contemplation," which leads to the deepening of his intellectual and spiritual life. The first few pictures depict his prenatal existence (where the tubercle bacillus looks like a pterodactyl, with a sharp beak and teeth), followed by his entrance into the world, where the angel of fate reads from a scroll describing his future: "This theory of pre-destination is probably a relic of my Scotch ancestors ... other angels ... as they read my future, turn away weeping." And the legend below reads "Restrain Not, Nor Should We, the Tribute of their Tears." In the third scene, he wonders whether measles, mumps, whooping cough, and diphtheria suffered in childhood have weakened him, leaving him vulnerable to tuberculosis. In the fifth drawing, he falls into an abyss of despair, comparable to Bunyan's Slough of Despond. In fact, much of "TB's Progress" is very similar to *The Pilgrim's Progress* and is a reminder of the kind of reading that Bethune must have done as a child. A heavy red river flows, representing a hemorrhage, but then the doctors are seen as the protection from his enemy, and music and laughter come out of the gates of the sanatorium as he returns to the city. In the seventh image the air is filled with TB in the form of bats who attack him again, and he has a relapse as "they swarm about the foetid air / while he grew sicker and sicker." In the ninth and last drawing he is held in the arms of death, whom he refers to as "thou kindest angel of them all." On a drawing of a tombstone, he writes 1932 as the year of his death.

But what really happened was typical of Bethune: he may have been in despair, but he was also busy researching advanced methods of treatment. He insisted that his doctor perform the then-radical method of artificial pneumothorax. It involved inserting a hollow needle into the patient's chest, pumping air into the chest cavity, thus pushing the lung to collapse and giving no opportunity for the tubercle bacilli to increase. In Bethune's case, this treatment successfully suppressed the tuberculosis, and he was able to leave the sanatorium before Christmas of 1927. "My life was saved by artificial pneumothorax," he wrote. "Looking back, I can see how my fears and hopeless attitude with regard to the future were wrong. Fear is the great destroyer of happiness, and most fears are unjustifiable."

A year later, established in Montreal, he wrote to Frances, from whom he was now divorced. "I will never return to general practice and am getting prepared to do nothing but chest work—both medical and surgical combined. The way will open out, I'm sure."

The way did open out, and in Montreal Bethune became one of the leading thoracic surgeons in North America.

It was defeating tuberculosis in himself that led Bethune to enter the field of thoracic surgery. Once there, he fought the disease on two fronts—as a doctor and as a social activist. He invented and had patents on twelve thoracic instruments, which were produced by George Pilling and Sons in Philadelphia. One of these, known as the Bethune Rib-Shears, is described in the catalogue as having "long handles, powerful biting jaws, suitable for all ribs including first rib." This awesome tool, or a form of it, is still in use.

He was a scientist with an inquiring mind, and he was willing to experiment. Surgery was in his view not only the application of scientific technique, but

> in all essentials ... a craft, and a surgeon [is] a craftsman, and an artisan.... Bound by the rigid and inexorable laws of his medium, the human body, the surgeon is permitted but few of the liberties his fellow craftsmen may take who work with stone, wood or metal. He is a master of make-shift, a ready compromiser, denied as in no other craft, the relief of substitution ... our craftsman often has the soul of the creative artist, although the nature of his plastic medium restricts the free play of his artistic nature. Like most other men, his creative force is consigned to one channel and allowed but one escape.

In his medical papers to specialized audiences, he was always optimistic and willing to admit that mistakes can be made by surgeons. He even presented a paper entitled "Twenty-five Howlers: Mistakes Made in Thoracic Surgery," unfortunately unpublished and now lost. Many procedures in medicine fail, and while Bethune's ego was large enough to be aggravating to his colleagues, it was also large enough for him to accept that mistakes could be recovered from. Bethune felt that surgeons, like all other human beings, could learn from their mistakes. The idea of the doctor as a kind of god was obviously not for him. He believed, as most surgeons believed, that he had to behave as if he were all-powerful in the operating room and in his decisions to go ahead with certain procedures, but he did not believe that surgeons were infallible. He was also aware that new instruments were being developed all the time and accepted that with inevitable further innovation, his inventions would be overtaken by others. The expansive ego and the scrupulous craftsman were well matched in Bethune; the portrayals of him in the 1970s in books and television and film lean too heavily on the idea of the manic, selfish, brilliant, uncontrollable person, when in fact all written evidence shows that he was able to strictly channel his strengths. He never avoided conflict, but he did not search it out needlessly either. He wasn't a careful person, but he was obviously able to decide when and where he was going to throw a fit.

Later, caught up in the civil war in Spain, in a foreign country where he did not speak the language, where he could not capture the nuances of what was going on, and where authority was pressuring him, he simply behaved badly. But in these Montreal years, in the practice of his profession, he was remarkable and was recognized as such.

Tuberculosis not only led him to his specialty in medicine, but formed his political and social views regarding poverty and its link to disease. He often repeated that "there are two kinds of tuberculosis—the rich man's and the poor man's. The rich man lives and the poor man dies." What he meant was that the rich could afford to go to exclusive sanatoria in the mountains to receive the rest, food, and change of air that could give them a chance of being cured. The poor were condemned to remain in the crowded, dirty conditions that bred the disease. Bethune saw this as an indictment of society, and it led him to re-evaluate the practice of medicine and identify as evil the gaining of profit from the treatment of patients.

CHAPTER FIVE

The Stormy Petrel

At the corner of Dorchester and Guy streets in Montreal, in the heart of Concordia University, there is an imposing statue of Norman Bethune on a two-metre-high pedestal. It has been there since 1976 at the centre of Bethune Square and is symbolic of how the city embraced him. Bethune's life in Montreal began in April 1928, when, at age thirty-eight, he was already an established thoracic surgeon. The city considers him its own, with some justification: it was in Montreal that he found the challenging intellectual milieu and grinding poverty that spurred him to commit his life to revolutionary change.

He endlessly told his friends there how much he had been influenced by his childhood on the Canadian Shield and the isolation he had shared with his fellow workers in the logging camps. It had been unbelievably rough—boxing matches with bare fists, bouts of drinking to senselessness, crude exploits with women whenever possible. Bethune, according to his friend and student Wendell MacLeod, identified with the Canadian Shield and continually mused about the muskeg, the lakes, the rocks.

The worldliness of Montreal, the city of a merchant class living in the Golden Square Mile, the most sophisticated city in Canada at the time, would have been both a release and a challenge for Bethune. Montreal the glamorous has always been the de facto capital of Canada. With its mountain and two rivers, its deep francophone culture, its Scottish efficiency, Irish energy, and Jewish dynamism, it held a strong allure for all Canadians.

After Bethune's two marriages to Frances Penney, his grave illness, and his basically unsatisfactory experience in Detroit, his earlier dream of being a rich surgeon in the United States now seemed to him to be hollow.

Bethune was asked to join the staff of the internationally renowned Royal Victoria Hospital, the teaching hospital of McGill University, by Dr. Edward Archibald, often called Canada's "father of pulmonary surgery." Quite deaf and rather absent-minded, Archibald shared with Bethune the trait of being late for everything. One of his colleagues wrote a poem in praise of him which ended with the lines "Oh, Edward you would be sublime, if only you could be on time." The deeply respected surgeon was also instrumental in recruiting the renowned neurosurgeon Wilder Penfield to

Montreal in the late 1920s. Archibald's was the hugely successful, highly traditional career of the eminent surgeon, and in hiring Norman Bethune he probably thought he was attracting a kindred spirit to the much-admired hospital.

All evidence suggests that Bethune was an impressive surgeon, not only when treating his patients, but also when helping to teach interns. It is typical of him as a man of action, and therefore a surgeon of action, that the first question he would ask about moderately or even advanced tuberculosis patients was "Should surgical operation be considered?" Bethune always insisted on investigating as deeply as possible to see whether there was any other cause of pulmonary infection, and he was sure to share his enthusiasm and discoveries with his interns. They and his nurses admired the way he treated patients with tenderness and consideration, sitting on their beds, explaining what would be done during the operation, what the odds were for living or dying, with or without surgery. He would then leave the decision in the hands of the patient by asking him or her to think it over and talk with him again in the morning. He would also engage the patient's family to gain their support and hear their concerns.

On the other hand, he often became irritated or enraged at interns or nurses. The mother of artist Christopher Pratt scrubbed for Bethune in his operating room and observed him shouting and throwing things. Nevertheless, she thought he was the finest doctor she ever knew. If there was any carelessness on the part of the staff in keeping records, he yelled or was brusque and impatient. In the face of what he considered to be obstinate stupidity, he reverted to behaving like the "put up your dukes" lumber foreman dealing with a recalcitrant worker. Wendell MacLeod describes him as being

> informal, outgoing, dynamic in speech and body movement, cheerful. He seemed to stimulate in us quickly a sense of person to person contact with him, a response evoked also from the patients he came to see for consultation. His gifts as a teacher came out most strikingly in the first of several weekly tutorials for the new interns.… He was very interested in how an issue or problem appeared to others, and pursued this before expressing crisply and dramatically his own view, which often was at variance with what was usually practiced or taught.

His effect on young interns was electric. He would ask them: "How often do you learn anything from palpation and percussion in routine examination? How often do heart and lung specialists disagree on what they percuss, or hear through the stethoscope? How often, in fact, do we discover early tuberculosis by physical examination?" The interns, who had just completed years of regimented and formalistic medical studies, loved his way of teaching and insisted on having more of his tutorials. He was also known for useful and simple innovations in keeping records of patients' progress, which were adapted by his colleagues.

Bethune, having been treated with great success by artificial pneumothorax, became one of the procedure's most enthusiastic and insistent supporters. He said, "No sanatorium today can call itself modern, which does not have at least 50% of its patients under some form of collapse therapy." And by the end of the 1930s, most Canadian sanatoria had attained that 50 percent goal.

Patients knew that he was interested in them and sympathetic. He was known to take money from his own pocket to reimburse them for the cost of taking public transport to visit him at the hospital. He shared his own experience of being tubercular with them. This care for patients—the traditional role of the physician—was noted everywhere he served as a doctor.

In these Montreal years, he seems to have been an impeccably caring surgeon, as well equipped to deal with the human side of drastic medical questions as he was with the technical challenges of surgery. His relationship to the young graduates was made more intense by the fact that he was only ten or fifteen years older than they were. He could look the part of a bourgeois doctor, with his clipped moustache and intense, inquiring gaze, and he used his brisk, commanding military manner to accomplish what he had to in a staid environment. But his life in Montreal also allowed him artistic expression, and he was being challenged intellectually and emotionally by the political currents of the time.

Initially, Archibald championed Bethune, but he came to regard the younger man's surgical technique as "quick, but rough, not careful, far from neat, and just a little dangerous!" In other words, Archibald, in many ways captive to the medical traditions of the time, albeit a brilliant exponent, came to distrust Bethune. And Bethune thought his chief was somewhat slow at operating and, perhaps because of that, also dangerous. Archibald was noted for taking things slowly, and some students used to joke that once he had made the opening incision, it was time for the assistants to have a tea break. Bethune believed that post-operative deaths occurred because the patient had been kept under anaesthesia for too long. Archibald would take two hours to perform a lobectomy. He took just under one.

Their mutual dislike grew, and Archibald later said, "I never really liked him; our outlook on life was too dissimilar … Bethune [was] … definitely abnormal, but not … a genius nor a leader.… He was an egocentric, his vision was keen but narrow. He wore blinkers … [and] trod on many toes quite often without knowing it or caring if he did know it. He had a superiority complex and he was entirely amoral."

The fact that Bethune changed his clothing as quickly as his moods was irritating to many as well. An apartment mate of his said that "his clothes [were] bought from the most expensive tailor in town … [he was] always insisting on white tie and tails at every appropriate occasion." He was just as capable, however, of going out to a party wearing shoes, trousers, and an overcoat but no shirt or jacket; once, in response to a dare, he dressed as a lumberjack to do his hospital rounds.

Undoubtedly he exuded the air of an impulsive and impatient man. But the general opinion was that he was a brilliant surgeon. He did make mistakes, which were of course what was remembered, but he acted as he did because he truly believed he could save more lives by his dramatic and sometimes risky surgical procedures. Many colleagues acknowledged, for example, that his high-risk procedures in operating on tubercular patients were justified by the fact that every case of open TB could, through infection, create ten more.

The daring and imagination that were the hallmarks of Bethune's character as a surgeon were the outgrowth of what he was as a personality. Whether he was an iconoclastic rebel or a superlatively brilliant surgeon, when the time came for him to leave the Royal Victoria Hospital, it was generally acknowledged both by his friends and his enemies that he simply did not fit in there.

Bethune was reaching the peak of his profession, writing and delivering numerous papers on his thoracic specialty all over North America, but he knew he could no longer work with Archibald. He was all but dismissed in the fall of 1932, and of course this hurt his reputation with the Montreal medical establishment. You simply did not leave the Royal Victoria Hospital; it was the promised land. If you had to leave, it was obviously your fault.

With Archibald's "recommendation" he was appointed to the Hôpital du Sacré-Coeur at Cartierville, on the outskirts of Montreal. Although he had left the glittering pinnacle, he was thrilled to be in charge of his own service. He wrote:

> I cauterized some adhesions there yesterday, and the chorus of oh's and ah's from the nuns rose like

a chant at the high altar. My title is *Chef dans le service du chirurgerie pulmonaire et de broncho-scopie.* I'm going to have a nice big white cap made with Chef marked in front. Really, I'm delighted.

The doctors at Sacré-Coeur were grateful to have such an internationally renowned colleague. Perhaps because of the cultural difference, they considered his eccentricities endearing rather than offensive. He was much admired by his colleagues for his professional work, especially by Dr. Georges Cousineau, who acted as his anaesthetist for most of his operations. Cousineau told Roderick Stewart that Bethune inspired the entire medical staff and did not send bills to patients. Bethune told him that, were he ever to establish a private practice again, he would simply leave an offering box at his door and his patients could pay whatever they could afford. Although he had expensive tastes, money was never an object in his life. He simply didn't care about it.

Bethune was doing well at Sacré-Coeur; he also became an associate member of the Association of Thoracic Surgery, frequently giving papers at their meetings. Yet he was not tamed by his acceptance into this medical establishment. He enraged the association when he criticized the low mortality rates some of the doctors boasted about in their papers. He pointed out that to achieve these results the doctors probably selected only favourable cases and suggested that they refused more risky operations to patients whose lives might have been saved. Naturally, this kind of talk gained him many enemies.

His time at Sacré-Coeur allowed Bethune to see how French-Canadian medicine worked and to be part of a team that lent its expertise to other hospitals in the province. With other doctors from the hospital he demonstrated techniques at the Hôpital Laval in Quebec and consulted for hospitals in cities such as Sherbrooke.

There was no question that Sacré-Coeur benefited from Bethune. They had a five-hundred-bed tuberculosis service, and the Sisters of Providence, who ran the hospital, wanted to change their morbid image as a place to dump incurables. At the same time, a lot of the young French-Canadian doctors were trying to create *une médecine québécoise* that would equal any in the world. This professional relationship was probably the happiest Bethune ever enjoyed. Here he was able to see French-Canadian patients cared for by excellent French-Canadian doctors, unlike at the Royal Vic, where the patients were frequently French-speaking but the entire medical establishment was anglophone. At this time in Montreal, only at Wilder Penfield's Montreal Neurological

Institute was there a concentrated administrative effort to bring representatives from the French-Canadian academic world into an anglophone medical institution. Perhaps having worked alongside non-English speakers in the lumber camps, Bethune instinctively put his best self forward to understand people who did not speak his language. The city of Montreal was divided into two solitudes, and Bethune took the opportunity to bridge that divide, not by language but by something just as deeply human—medical care.

Many observers of Bethune's life considered his time at Sacré-Coeur to have been somehow a step down for him. The most generous explanation for this attitude is that they simply knew nothing about the French-Canadian medical establishment. The prejudices of the time would have led them to believe that no good work could possibly happen in a francophone Catholic hospital to equal that of the lofty anglophone McGill and its revered teaching hospital. But it's typical of Bethune that he found himself in a situation that to others was unpromising but in which he was able to commit his energies and create something of value.

Besides performing his duties as a surgeon and advocating for compression therapy, he was writing articles, radio plays, poetry, and short stories, a number of which were broadcast and published. He was also painting seriously, taking lessons from Edwin Holgate, and executed a self-portrait in oils as a very proper gentleman-doctor with tie and jacket.

He worked very much on intuition, understanding situations through feeling and emotions. He frequently told people, "I am an artist," meaning not just his efforts as a painter and as a poet but also his work as a doctor. Nothing could be further from the world of academic and conventionally practised medicine. He wrote:

> A great artist lets himself go. He is natural. He swims easily in the stream of his own temperament. He listens to himself. He respects himself. He has a deeper fund of strength to draw from than that arising from rational and logical knowledge....
>
> The function of the artist is to disturb. His duty is to arouse the sleeper, to shake the complacent killers of the world. He reminds the world of its dark ancestry, shows the world its present and points the way to its new birth. He is at once the product and the preceptor of his time.... In a world terrified of change, he preaches revolution—the principle of life. He is an agitator, a dis-

turber of the peace—quick, impatient, positive, restless and disquieting. He is the creative spirit of life, working in the soul of men.

When we look at his paintings, from the earliest tuberculosis mural to portraits of himself and others, it's obvious that he could have been a very good artist had he given it the time and devotion it required. He was frequently in the company of artists such as John Lyman, Paraskeva Clark, Frederick Taylor, and Anne Savage. The apocalyptic, volcanic tone of his declarations about art indicates a romanticism that was never far below the surface of his personality. This romanticism took a flamboyant form that was almost childlike in its enjoyment of shock and would underlie his profound belief in the revolutionary.

He focused a lot of his energies on trying to develop artistic skill in others, believing that to evoke the artist in each person was to evoke something essential and profound. Early in 1936, he began two initiatives that show his passion for art and medicine. The first was to establish the Montreal Children's Creative Art Centre in his own apartment at Beaver Hall Square, where he offered classes three afternoons a week and on Saturday mornings. The apartment had been previously rented to the artists Jean Palardy and Jean-Paul

Lemieux. In the words of one friend: "It was a spacious flat, renovated by owners to be rented out as architectural studios but Bethune made the most renovations and in the large front room was the studio with a kitchen a few steps up and a balcony facing west where sunflowers grew in pots ... [it was furnished] with taste, but very little money." He asked his friend artist Fritz Brandtner to direct the art centre. Marian Dale Scott, who was one of the instructors, described the motivation: "Beth always had this very strong feeling that children ... could come and work with colours and be free to draw and express their ideas or feelings, that this might even affect them later on when they faced hardships."

The children were asked to spread paper all over the floor and just paint whatever they liked. It was far from the method of the schools of the time, which required that houses had roofs and doors and that trees had green leaves. For Bethune, who in the Presbyterian household of his youth had never been encouraged to express himself so freely, this was a delight. You feel that the child in Bethune was projecting itself onto these needy children. The lessons were intended to open their minds to a world beyond the slums, the garbage, the smell of poverty. On Saturdays they would be taken by Brandtner or Bethune to museums or art galleries or to see attractive buildings; they would go for walks and later paint what they had seen or experienced. One of the children, Sylvia Ary, became a painter. She recalled that the children all loved Bethune, who used to give them special treats and talk to them about what they were seeing and let them express what they felt.

At the same time, in 1936, Bethune was working to promote a better understanding of the connection between poverty and public health. He made speeches at medical congresses and gave public lectures to emphasize the relationship between poverty and disease, but his views were shared by very few of his colleagues. Together with George Mooney, a YMCA secretary, he opened a free medical clinic in the Montreal suburb of Verdun on Saturdays. It was Bethune's response to his own profession's devotion to profit and the government's indifference to suffering. The Depression after the stock market crash of 1929 had brought with it untold misery to millions in North America. Many intellectuals and professionals saw that suffering and decided that fundamental change was needed. Many believed that socialism was the answer, and some questioned whether free-market capitalism was even moral, its having demonstrated since the Industrial Revolution its capacity for brutalizing human beings.

Bethune insisted in one of his speeches that

> in our highly geared modern industrial society there is no such thing as private health, all health is public. The ill and maladjustment of one unit of the mass affects all other members. The protection of the people's health should be recognized by the government as its primary obligation and duty to its citizens.

He went on to say that medicine would have to be completely reorganized, welded into an army of doctors, nurses, social workers, technicians. And he exhorted doctors to

> take the profit, the private economic profit, out of medicine and purify our profession of rapacious individualism. Let us make it disgraceful to enrich ourselves at the expense of the miseries of our fellow man. Let us organize ourselves so that we can no longer be exploited as we are being exploited by our politicians. Let us redefine medical ethics, not as a code of professional etiquette between doctors but as a code of fundamental morality and justice between medicine and the people.

It's too bad we don't have any record of how the doctors reacted to this, but we can guess. A doctor who had invited him to speak in Memphis noted afterwards that "it was my impression that he laid it on somewhat thicker than he actually felt because he was thoroughly enjoying the reaction of his audience."

Bethune had witnessed Montreal police brutally attack unemployed demonstrators, and perhaps that pushed him into believing there was no room for gradual social reform, that the shock of revolution was necessary. Though Bethune was fairly sympathetic to the aims of the League of Social Reconstruction—the intellectual incubator of the newly formed Co-operative Commonwealth Federation (or CCF, precursor of the NDP)—he felt that they were a lukewarm group. He wrote that he was

> *profoundly* distrustful of social democracy and of the CCF, in their non-realization of the absolute inevitability of the use of force and force alone as the only true persuader.
>
> Monied people will never give up money and power until subjugated by physical forces stronger than they possess. Democracy will come again, as it will come again in Russia, only after the people are conditioned, as they are being conditioned, to their new manner of living, but democracy at first

is shiftless, careless, ignorant and willful. Only when the course is set can it be permitted to guide the ship.

Yet he pulled back from committing himself to the Communist Party. When asked about it by a Communist friend in 1935, he replied:

> What stands in my way of non-acceptance? *This*—my strong feeling of individualism—the right of a man to walk alone, if that's his nature—my dislike of crowds and regimentation. Perhaps all these fears are illusionary and do not necessarily conflict with the practice of Communism ... but the ironic and ludicrous picture of a half-hearted convert, reluctantly being burnt at the stake for his half-hearted, feeble convictions, rises in my mind. So it all hinges on this—I am not ready as yet to throw my lot in with you.

It was George Mooney, his YMCA friend, who persuaded Bethune to go to the Soviet Union to see for himself what revolution could do.

In August 1935, he attended the International Physiological Congress in Moscow and Leningrad. The renowned Russian behavioural scientist Dr. Ivan Pavlov (he of the bells and salivating dogs) was a key speaker. Dr. Hans Selye, who would later become the great specialist on the effects of stress, also went to the Congress, as did Bethune's fellow graduate Dr. Frederick Banting. They wanted to find out whether things really were better under the Soviet system; though rosy pictures had been drawn by other visitors, they were skeptical. But Bethune did discover that in the Soviet Union all children were tested to detect early tuberculosis, that there were halfway homes for convalescents from tuberculosis who were beginning to work again, and that there were medical stations in factories. He also felt that the Russian love of children was superbly manifested in the Soviet daycare system, which was not rigid and formulaic but full of warmth and laughter.

On Bethune's return from Russia, one friend noted that he was "composed, quietly confident, patient, tolerant of others' views.... He seemed to be contented, optimistic about the future.... Integrative forces seem to be at work in his thinking." He told his friends he had seen great advances in Soviet Russia and was deeply impressed by their system of hospitalization, welfare, and social medicine. Typically, he exaggerated his approval of what he had seen in order to

overcome his irritation at the hostile anti-communist feelings he found on his return.

Stanley Ryerson, the secretary of the Quebec division of
the Communist Party, tells us that having joined the party
in November 1935, Bethune found in Communist theory
"the difference between bohemian gesture and revolutionary dedication: between theatrical posturing and affirma-
tion of life." His readings gave him a solid intellectual
background for what he was already naturally inclined to
believe: that the individual entered history and had a
relationship with it rather than simply living alongside it.
This was the great moving force behind the last three years
of his life. By living a real and authentic life, the individual
enters history not as somebody who deliberately chooses to
change it or to dominate it but as someone who lives
within the movements that express and validate his own
character.

Bethune attended meetings of a "closed" group of
Communists during the winter of 1936 together with
artists, teachers, accountants, and social workers. The meetings were held in different people's homes and were secret:
the Communist Party of Canada was an illegal organization
(from 1931 to 1936 under section 98 of the Federal
Criminal Code; then from 1937 to 1956 under the Quebec

Act to Protect the Province Against Communistic Propaganda, the so-called Padlock Law; and from 1939 to 1942 under the War Measures Act). The Padlock Law was enacted specifically to target the Communist Party, because it authorized the arbitrary search of homes and premises and the confiscation of documents. It could be used against any person the government termed radical, and the subject party, whether an owner of a private home or hall or a member of a meeting, was denied the usual presumption of innocence.

Why, given his dislike of "regimentation," was Bethune willing to submit himself to a collective activity? One observer, also a surgeon, compared Bethune to a stormy petrel, the seabird used figuratively to describe a person who delights in strife or whose appearance is a harbinger of bad weather. Certainly in his choices he was a herald of things to come. Bethune always forged ahead; he never followed. Perhaps an answer to the question of how Bethune could be part of a collective is that when he decided to give himself, he gave himself entirely. And he had more to give than most.

An address he made in April 1936 was entitled "Take the Private Profit Out of Medicine," and it was a logical outcome of his previously stated ideals.

Medicine must be envisaged as embedded in the social fabric and inseparable from it. It is the product of any given social environment. The basis of any social structure is economic. The economic theory and practice in this country is termed capitalistic. It is founded on individualism, competition and private profit. This capitalistic system is undergoing an economic crisis—commonly called the Depression. This is not a temporary illness of the body politic, but a deadly disease requiring systemic treatment…. Medicine, as we are practicing it, is a luxury trade. We are selling bread at the price of jewels. The poor, which comprise 50% of our population, cannot pay and starve; we cannot sell and suffer.

There were, he told his audience, "only three great economic groups in Canada, the comfortable, the uncomfortable, and the miserable." He pointed out the "appalling fact" that "38.2% of all people irrespective of income receive no medical, dental, or eye care whatsoever … 25 years ago it was thought contemptible to be called a Socialist. Today it is ridiculous not to be one. Medical reforms such as limited health insurance schemes are not socialized medicine. They are bastard forms of socialism produced by belated humani-tarianism out of necessity."

The Montreal Group for the Security of the People's Health, a small organization of like-minded teachers, social workers, and medical personnel founded by Bethune, was preparing a detailed plan for a system of state medical care. Quebec was on the verge of its second provincial election within a year. Louis-Alexandre Taschereau had resigned, and Adélard Godbout, the new Liberal premier, had called an election for August 17, 1936. The group rushed to make its proposal public before the election was held. It was sent to all fifty candidates in Montreal; to Premier Godbout; and to Maurice Duplessis, the leader of the Opposition. Copies were sent to all the medical, dental, and nursing professions and to social and charitable agencies. In it the group suggested a new health care plan to be implemented on a small scale for a trial period and proposed that, on the basis of the results, a plan for the entire province could be formulated. It included

> *A system of municipally financed medicine.* One Montreal hospital would be selected for which all staff members would be salaried. The hospital would be subjected to close scrutiny to determine

costs in order that it be placed on a sound actuarial basis.

Compulsory health insurance. An entire community would pay health insurance to determine actual costs and the ability of the community to meet the costs.

Voluntary health insurance. This would be offered in one community of five to ten thousand people.

Care for the unemployed. This would be adopted on a fee-for-service basis throughout the Province of Quebec, to be financed from taxation.

This proposal was met with resounding indifference from the medical profession, the political class, and the public; anything that smacked of publicly funded health care carried with it the subtext of Russian Communism and was not looked upon kindly.

Bethune was perhaps most disappointed by his fellow doctors. They did get some serious support from an editorial in the Montreal *Gazette*, which talked about the lack of advance in public health and put the blame on the economic conditions in which the majority of the population found themselves. It came out for compulsory health insurance, but, tellingly, at no point was the Montreal group referred to by name.

To Bethune this was a great personal blow. As a surgeon, he could make people pay attention because what he was doing was a matter of life and death, but he had now run up against the self-interest of his fellow doctors and their wish to enrich themselves through medical practice. He thought this was immoral and said so.

Of his time in Montreal, the years 1935 and 1936 were the most intense. He had worked hard to achieve something for public health with a group of like-minded professionals; he had founded his children's art centre; he had established the free medical clinic in Verdun; he had continued to paint and write poetry and short stories. Throughout, he retained an ability to base what he did and believed on the real situation, not on abstraction or bias or self-interest. Though he accepted membership in the Communist Party, he remained, as his biographer Larry Hannant so graphically put it, "a humanist in a red cape." But Bethune was jolted into action by his disappointment, which several months later would lead to his departure for Spain.

CHAPTER SIX

A Tiger of Sweetness, of Fierceness and Delight

There were many women in Bethune's life—and he loved some of them—but womanizing was not something that pre-occupied him. If women threw themselves in his way, he availed himself of them as emergency sexual rations. He loved women, but he didn't attempt to conquer them. His friend Libby Park, who worked with him in the Montreal Group for the Security of People's Health, said that she liked his attitude toward women because he didn't have stereotyped male atti-tudes about them; to him, a woman was a person with a mind and a personality. If he was arguing with a woman, he never made allowances for her sex, and if he disagreed, he didn't do so with a condescending attitude. His nurse in China, Jean Ewen, confirmed this. Park knew some of the women who passed through Bethune's life, and she noted that he

> said he loved women passionately and made love
> with some. Women I have known who were in

love with Norman have spoken of him in very different terms.… For me the word 'womanizer' so often used in connection with him vulgarizes Norman Bethune's attitude towards women and in no way captures the kinds of relationships that existed between him and women who were often friends and sometimes lovers.

He was brilliant, difficult, and highly entertaining to be with. He never sought to destroy anyone through his sexual power. In the Montreal of his time, Norman Bethune cut a great figure: first of all, he was a revolutionary doctor in every sense. He was dramatically undomesticated. He went with friends to dime-a-dance places and with his flatmate Aubrey Geddes threw parties that brought together artistic as well as medical colleagues. One male artist friend recalled,

I was drawn to him by his keen intelligence, forceful personality and intensity.… As he drank he became increasingly irascible and difficult.… He picked arguments and insulted people everywhere we went.… It devolved upon me to get him out of a good many fights, some of them quite nasty, and to get him home.

The years 1934 and 1935 were good ones for Bethune. His friends found him vigorous, involved, and optimistic. In 1934 his Christmas card, a clever caricature he had sketched of his own invention for decompression, wished everybody "a Happy Pneumothorax."

In the summer of 1935, when he set off for the Soviet Union to attend the International Physiological Congress, Bethune found himself on board ship with Marian Dale Scott and her six-year-old son, Peter. They had already met in Montreal at the home of the artist John Lyman, who, with Scott, had been a founding member of Montreal's Contemporary Arts Society. Bethune "seemed to me essentially the pioneer, impatient with travel, with things that had been done before," Scott would later tell Ted Allan, "but then that is just another way of saying that he was an artist, isn't it?" They continued to see each other in London before he travelled on to the Soviet Union, intensely discussing art, poetry, and politics. He fell deeply in love with her and a profound and intimate relationship developed. Bethune's nickname for Scott was Pony. She was to be the unique love of his life.

Not only was Pony married, but she was married to constitutional lawyer F.R. Scott, one of the leading intellectuals and poets of the day, whose socialist views and legal prowess made him a formidable figure in Montreal. He wrote the founding documents of the CCF, fought the Padlock Law for years and successfully had it struck down, and in his old age became a trusted adviser to Pierre Elliott Trudeau. Part of the anglophone establishment of Montreal, Marian was brought up with governesses and often spent summer holidays in England with family, some of whom she was visiting when she made her trip in 1935 with her son.

Scott won a scholarship to the Montreal Arts Association's School of Art, but while she knew she wanted to be an artist, she also longed to lead a traditional life. She was the respectable lady her mother had wanted her to be, albeit a bluestocking. She was very beautiful—as we see in television interviews she gave later in life. She was remarkable for the delicacy of her bone structure and the classical perfection of her features, which was relieved by a hint of irony playing around her mouth as she politely answered questions. She had wide intellectual interests. Through her reading, which included theologians such as Thomas à Kempis, she searched for the way of life she would choose to lead.

Bethune's and Scott's similar religious backgrounds (her grandfather was a Presbyterian minister) would have made for a common understanding of values. In her work Scott dealt with spiritual subjects, one of which, the burning bush, fascinated her. The image of the bush that burns but is not consumed by flame is an intriguing one when we think of Scott and her relationship to Bethune.

She married Frank Scott in 1928, at the age of twenty-two. Her husband respected her desire to lead her own life, but while she promised herself in her diary that she would develop all her intellectual capacities, she nevertheless chastised herself for not being a good housekeeper: "There are holes in Peter's socks and cobwebs on the ceiling corners and my skirt is much too long so I leave my painting and come down to earth." She was in fact an assiduous hostess; menus and shopping lists abound in her diaries. Frank and Marian Scott each decided in their own way to give each other room to be autonomous and free. Marian once said that "creative spirits needed varied experiences ... especially men!" She recognized and accepted the fact that Frank had extra-marital adventures and observed in her diary that "men are polygamous and faithful at the same time and we must accept this and not feel that we are personally put into question by it." Still, his infidelity wounded her self-esteem, and she felt that equality among men and women was impossible under these conditions, that women were inclined to give everything of themselves and were then left "empty." She wrote about the insecurity this caused her: "This pain is ... a flowering from within so that I may get my satisfaction from rich giving rather than from taking from others." She had not at this point produced a great deal of art; she was clinging to the idea of artistic creation as a way of establishing her identity and dealing with the contradictions in her marriage.

Then she found herself on board the same steamship to Europe as Norman Bethune: "Managed the take-off quite well. I was pretty tired and [that] was probably the reason of my nursing of my suffering from sea-sickness today—I have enjoyed today—mainly due to Dr. Bethune whom I had always heard of as a black sheep and who I had met once very drunk at the Lymans—I like him and like him very much to talk to—you don't have to begin at the beginning with him—you are really talking right away at least so it was today."

He was reading poetry on the trip, particularly William Blake. Poetry bound Bethune and Scott closer together; by the time they got to England, he was passionately in love with her. He drew a poster, which he sent her in London. The text read:

Lost

In the neighbourhood of Ecclestone Square, on July 17th, a Canadian bred Pony accompanied by foal stands about five and a half hands high. White face, gentle disposition.

Was the companion of a small boy, who is inconsolable over his loss. Any information received leading to her recovery will be handsomely rewarded. Address—Beth, c/o Canada House.

When Bethune and Scott were both back in Montreal, he wrote the following letter.

Pony,

It is pleasant to sit and think that you are near me, close beside me, only a few streets away. I am very conscious of your presence and happy because of it—yet sad too, because of the knowledge that you and I are bound together to work out some part of our lives together—for good or for evil—we seem to be bound.

Perhaps this is a presumption on my part—but I think not. And if your glance, your touch, your hands and lips are not mistaken, unreal or misread—you feel it too.

Do you remember the girl in *Farewell to Arms* [Hemingway's 1929 novel] saying with that mysterious foresight of love "Let us be good to each other. We are to have such a strange life together." And her lover comforts her sad heart as best he can, not knowing or understanding. But she knew the dark paths ahead.

Well, my sweet, I know it too.

Let me persuade you to stop now.

Go back. Put away this small child of our love you are holding so quietly and tenderly in your cupped hand—now, when it can be put away without agony and tears—before it has grown in stature and strength and threatens to destroy all you hold precious in life—your home, your husband, your child.

And I say this because I am persuaded there is something fatal and doomed and predestined about myself (and I know it). [The last four words are crossed out.]

But again I think—no. Let us go on into the future together—heads up and with a smile on our lips. If we are true to ourselves, the future may not be happy (oh Pony I'm afraid, so afraid for you)—but no real harm or injury can touch us—nothing can come from without to destroy us. This is the way I tried to persuade myself and you.

It is because I love you I write like this, so darkly, lest I injure you with my love and do you harm. In the name of love and life instead of bedecking you with jewels I load you with chains.

Beth your sad lover

This love was reciprocated, and the correspondence and many poems from Bethune that followed show a desire both to possess and to nobly renounce.

Bethune and Scott were weighing the consequences of a full-blown love affair. And for those who might think it was unlike Bethune not to avail himself of a beautiful woman once she had crossed his path, it must be noted that the object of his love was unusual and self-aware; she was an artist, a mother, the wife of someone he could not have helped respecting, and he understood the struggle she was having with herself. Besides, Marian Scott loved her husband: there is no evidence in anything she wrote or is known to have done that belies this. It must have been extremely difficult for her to be in love with two such extraordinary men.

Scott and Bethune both withdrew at the same time, knowing the consequences of going further could shatter four lives—Marian's, Frank's, Peter's, and Bethune's.

In September 1935, Scott drafted letters to him in her journal that often have a chaotic feel to them: "You must find some centre of interest which is all important around which the focus of life may be gathered. This centre, once found, other virtues may be built about it…. You will always crave experience, romantic adventure, growth and change excitement even struggle." And later that week: "I am happy, impervious to those who came before, those to come after, for you, a complicated unsatisfied creature, [we] recognize each other and know that because we are what we are, we need each other."

They spent a great deal of time in those autumn months discussing what the nature of their relationship would be and whether they would truly become lovers; they were obviously wrestling with the situation. When Bethune was laid up with a case of jaundice he sent Scott a drawing of himself in his sickbed reading from a volume of Karl Marx. And in November he wrote her this moving but somewhat manipulative assessment of what their relationship meant.

Pony—these are some of the things I've been thinking since I received your letter this morning.

I, this person you love, am nothing. Understand that firmly. I am nothing in myself. I represent and symbolize an emotion emanating from yourself—of your own being. I am merely an externalized part of your own vital self. We could have gone a long way together ... if we had held each other's hands.

I have been robbed of jewels.

The tyranny of love, of old love, is holding you. Your emergent and evolutionary spirit is being blackmailed by the past....

You need more children. You need an altar to immolate yourself upon—a glad, burning sacrifice to a living god—you ask to be consumed, to rise again like a phoenix from the ashes of your own glad destruction—clean, pure and free—with wings.

I'll make no effort to urge. Be sure of that. You must do what you must do. Acting under the urge of an inner compulsion, your motives and actions must be pure and direct.

I was sad, yet glad when you left on Monday. I saw you as a wall closing in again on me—a loving wall!—and I raised my head, restless. Oh God, I said to myself, must I go thru it all again—the ecstasy and agony of love.

I am solitary, loving privacy, my own satisfactory aloneness. I saw you as a threat to this. I didn't need any woman or any man … a straight glance, a firm hand—a plea—'I love you, I want you'—is what a man or a woman should make to his mate. Otherwise he has merely shifted his position physiologically and anatomically and not spiritually—from the womb, from the breast, from the arms—back to arms and breast again—the eternal child—chronic infantilism…. You turned to me as an instrument upon which to play your song of psalms—your life-song of love—then found you didn't want to sing!

As far as I am concerned, I am the only person alive in the world. Other people—men and women—are to me canvas, interesting animated 'things'—but not more important or not readily distinguishable from rocks, trees, wind, rain, sun and water (I could swim in you)…. So I don't need you (except to bathe in and bask in!). I want you as a man wants a woman…. I like you rather like I like myself…. You are my sister—we think alike, act alike, and feel alike. I am merely the masculine edition of yourself. You are the first woman in the world I have met without whom I have felt no doubt that we could live together, physically and mentally and spiritually mated. This has never happened to me before and is important.

I am glad now we did not take each other physically. For me it would have meant that I would not have left you, as I am leaving you now ... I should have behaved with most unseemly vigour, and lack of manners, shouts and clamours. And for you it was as well too. You have now the exquisite sense of virtue preserved, of moral rectitude.... You are still a faithful wife. And if you had, what then—for a thirst appeased, a hunger satisfied, but with your conflict, your essential problem unchanged, so for you no serenity, no peace, no quietness of soul. And because I would know this instantly, neither for me either serenity, peace or quietness.

... Well, Pony, my sweet, all this is to say I love you, I want you and I respect you.

I am here if I can be of any use to you at any time and that's all one man can say to a woman. Au revoir. Beth

This renunciation in November, which coincided with Bethune's joining the Communist Party, was not sustained. A month later, just before Christmas 1935, he wrote, "Oh Pony, Pony—it was false. I do need you. Beth." And the day after Christmas, he wrote, "Pony, darling, I adore you. Come and take tea with me Friday afternoon. Beth who loves you."

On January 10, Scott writes in her diary: "B feels the only way to escape from the monotony of day by day—from the mundane is by violence, by excess, but I feel the surer way is slow evolution—B feels always the danger—boredom biting at his heels.... B's life is tide—it rises and ebbs slowly wearing away the pebbles, mine is a slow unspectacular climb almost circular but never quite touching the same place—a spiral."

At this time they were both involved with the Children's Creative Art Centre; this gave them something they could share and that touched their emotional as well as their artistic lives. Scott confided to her journal on March 11: "As I grow older I become more vivid—every year life becomes more valuable and my self-respect grows and my belief in what I can achieve grows." Norman Bethune's love for her gave her a true sense of her own worth, and this in turn helped her to create the art she knew she was capable of. In

May, she addressed Bethune in her journal: "I would so like to prove to Frank and to myself that there can be a worthwhile relationship between a man and a woman without the sexual consummation.… No, you are not a lion really—a tiger of sweetness, of fierceness and delight, does it mean something to you when I come to see you—to me it's something like music or … colours."

On October 17, 1936, two weeks before going to Spain, Bethune wrote her a one-line letter: "Goodbye Pony the world has been a fine place to live in because of you Beth." On October 22 she confided:

> More moved than I knew I could be by Beth's goodbye letter—somehow didn't believe he was really going the other night.
>
> Don't know whether to try and see him before he goes—would like to see him to tell him how fond I am of him to tell him how I respect him and have found him one of the two nicest people I have known—that if my behaviour has seemed strange considering this, it is only because I must abide by my own decision.… I might write a letter but if I send it he may not be there.

She made notes for a letter to him: "I haven't really been able to put my mind to anything probably because of [your going to Spain] you don't know how I hate that you are going and yet it's what I want to do myself I think. Instead of feeling unhappy I suppose I should try to make it a spur into finding a way of life for myself but I want you to know that I respect—you."

There is a kind of passionate and fiery elegance to the way in which Marian Dale Scott and Norman Bethune accept the renunciation of a great love which might have changed the course of their lives. Would he have gone to Spain? Probably, yes. Would he have gone to China? Again, most likely, yes. For all the strength it gave them, their love would probably not have changed the direction of his life, and it might ultimately have ruined hers. Her notes suggest she knew that.

Marian Scott became a fine artist; her work lives on and is much admired. In 2000, seven years after her death, the Musée de Québec held a major retrospective. In her paintings, she managed to reconcile her deepest spiritual feelings with her iconoclastic vision of what art could be. Norman Bethune had warned her that he didn't need anyone and that he considered himself "the only person alive in the world." He always had the sense that he was set apart and that an ordinary life would never be for him. Probably he was as shocked and surprised by his love for Scott as she was by him. In the end, they did not risk everything on this relationship, and so it remained a rocky, forested island in the increasingly turbulent waters of this man's life.

En route to Spain he sent a telegram recalling the Blake poem they had read on the ship together to England: "Pony do you remember oh Rose thou art Sick the invisible worm which rides in the wind and the howling storm hath found out thy bed of crimson joy and his secret love both doth thy life destroy [signed] The Sick Rose."

No further intimate correspondence exists. The Scott marriage endured: Frank Scott died in 1985 and Marian Dale Scott in 1993.

CHAPTER SEVEN

Those Who in Their Lives Fought for Life

The cause of the legally elected Republican government in Spain roused the democratic egalitarian in Bethune, as it did in so many of his contemporaries in North America and Europe. Bethune declared, "It is in Spain that the real issues of our time are going to be fought out. It is there that democracy will either die or survive."

Before his departure in October 1936, Bethune wrote a poem entitled "Red Moon," which was published in the *Canadian Forum* the following July.

> And this same pallid moon tonight,
> which rides so quietly, clear and high,
> the mirror of our pale and troubled gaze,
> raised to the cool Canadian sky,
> Above the Spanish mountain tops,
> last night rose low and wild and red,
> reflecting back from her illumined shield,

the blood bespattered faces of the dead.
To that pale disc we raise our clenched fists
and to those nameless dead our vows renew,
"comrades who fought for freedom in the future
world,
who died for us, we will remember you."

He also composed a will, in which he left his flat at Beaver Hall Square, all its contents, and his account at the Royal Bank to his former wife, Frances. He also gave her power of attorney and asked that $300 be paid to her by a friend, Dr. Hy Shister. As founder of the Children's Creative Art Centre, he wanted his estate to fund the centre for four months.

He sent the following note to artist Charles Comfort:

<u>Epitaph</u> (for future) Norman Bethune
<u>Rx</u> Born a bourgeois
<u>Died a Communist</u>

The note was headed with a sketch of the Republican flag and underneath it were the words "Long live the revolution!"

On November 3, Bethune arrived in Madrid, just before a huge offensive was unleashed by General Francisco Franco's army against the Republican city. It is hard for us now to imagine the chaos surrounding events in Spain. The Republican government had been elected in 1936. The Spanish army stationed in Spain's North African colonies rebelled under the leadership of General Franco. On July 18, 1936, he broadcast a manifesto from Palma, Majorca, which led to military uprisings on the Spanish mainland. Hitler provided Franco with the Condor Legion of 5,000 airmen and 100 bombers and fighter planes; Mussolini sent an expeditionary force of 50,000—four full divisions. Many, like Bethune, believed that if fascism could be stopped in Spain, a larger war would not break out. France was governed by its first socialist government, under Léon Blum. Europe was sharply divided between the Left and the Right. Neutrality provisions passed by the League of Nations barred its members, including Canada and the United States, from intervening, but at least 40,000 men and women from more than 60 countries were making their way to Spain to serve the Republican government as members of the International Brigade. Nearly 1,200 Canadians were to be part of the Mackenzie-Papineau Battalion, which would go into action in the summer of 1937, but Bethune was already operating at the front in November 1936. Initially he thought that he would simply serve as a doctor. There was a shortage of doctors on the Republican side because most of the army medical corps had gone with the fascists, but there was no pre-assigned role for him.

Bethune did not speak any foreign languages, but neither here nor later in China did this seem to make him any less effective or limit his ability to communicate and use his medical skills. He had a volunteer interpreter, Henning Sorensen, a Danish Canadian who spoke a number of languages and later went to work as a translator in the Cuban ministry of foreign affairs after Fidel Castro became president in 1959.

Bethune could have worked at any number of hospitals, where his skills as a surgeon would have guaranteed his usefulness, but he realized quickly where the most pressing needs lay. In his usual way, he came to the rapid and imaginative conclusion that a mobile blood transfusion unit was needed in Spain to bring blood to the wounded in the field. He must have recalled his own experience as a stretcher-bearer in Flanders during the First World War, when the wounded could not get transfusions in time. To bring blood to the field of battle was not a new idea, but it had never been put into practice.

But now that he had the idea, how was he going to execute it? He took Sorensen with him to Paris and to London, and within a month they were back in Madrid with a young

Canadian architect who had been living in London. Hazen Sise came from a wealthy, prominent family in Montreal (his father was president of the Northern Electric Company). Sise had already visited Spain before the Civil War broke out; he liked the country and its people and considered Spain's Republican government, elected by a considerable majority in 1936, as being slightly to the right of Mackenzie King's Liberal government in Canada.

As soon as Bethune met Sise in London, he gave him a description of what an enormously moving spectacle Madrid was—a city whose citizens had mobilized themselves in resistance and were throwing up barricades on the streets and fighting in the suburbs. At that point Spain had a small Communist Party, with no particular power or profile, but in response to Franco's invasion, the trade unions in Madrid and Barcelona were arming themselves as fast as they could and organizing themselves into military units. When Bethune indicated that he was in London to buy medical supplies and was going back in a few days' time, Sise said, "I wish I could go with you." Bethune thought it over and in the morning said that Sise could help him buy a car and drive down with him to Madrid, at which point, if he didn't want to stay, he could go back to London, no hard feelings. They were racing to get to Madrid before the fascists closed in around the city.

Miraculously, Madrid held out for another two and a half years, until the very end of the war in 1939. For Sise, Bethune's vivid personality was irresistible. Sise recalled in 1976: "He was literally the sort of person who could say 'rise and follow me' and you would follow him. He had that sort of authority about him."

Bethune knew very little about blood transfusion, and before they left London Sise saw him reading textbooks on the subject late into the night. The car they bought was a modest Ford station wagon with wooden sides. Inside was a refrigerator that operated on coal oil; it later turned out that the refrigerator was a mistake because it could not be very accurately controlled; there was danger of freezing the blood in it.

As they drove through France, they feared that they might be sabotaged by one of the right-wing paramilitary organizations in the country. On the side of the car they had affixed a crude, handmade sign indicating that they were a Canadian blood transfusion service. They got waved through. Down the Rhône Valley to the south, groups of people working on the roads would stand and raise their clenched fists in the socialist salute and cheer them on. At the proletarian level, the support was certainly very strong. Sise, a talented photographer, took pictures of their journey, to Perpignan, in the south of France, and crossing over into Spain. Now everybody they met on the road raised their clenched fists in salute. When they had repairs made to the car in Barcelona by the anarchist trade union, the Confederación Nacional del Trabajo, the workers refused payment.

They drove into the bowl-shaped city of Madrid on November 20 and stayed for several days at a hotel until they took up residence in a large apartment. The only diplomatic contact they had was with the British Embassy, which received Sise in a hostile fashion, urging him to leave immediately because Madrid was going to fall. Sise believed the British really hoped Madrid would fall. He and Bethune felt the British and the Americans wanted Franco to win, because the left—whether socialist or communist—was anathema to them. The two Canadians stayed clear of the British and American establishment.

English and Scottish sympathizers of the Republican cause had organized a hospital and an ambulance service. Bethune wanted to make a specifically Canadian contribution, and to that end he called his program Servicio Canadiense de Transfusión de Sangre. Their apartment had previously been occupied by a German diplomat and was protected by the Socorro Rojo Internacional (SRI, or International Red Aid), which was connected to the Communist International. Like many on the left, Bethune suspected the International Red Cross of being pro-fascist and considered the Spanish Red Cross very weak. Because the SRI had been formed to help the families of those whom the fascists had persecuted, he found them very sympathetic. His initial group included Sorensen, Sise, two Spanish medical students, a Spanish biologist, and Celia Ceborer Greenspan, a nurse from New York.

Bethune realized how important it was to have a separate unit so that Canadians could focus on what they were supporting when they gave money to the Canadian Committee to Aid Spanish Democracy. He also knew instinctively that collecting blood, something literally visceral, would hold a very primitive and powerful appeal for the Spanish people. This is an example of Bethune's plugging straight into the collective unconscious and understanding instinctively that the Spanish people would take the unit to their hearts. The response was indeed strongly emotional.

Bethune, with his sense of public relations, cultivated friends among influential foreign correspondents in Spain, such as Herbert Matthews of *The New York Times*. The Canadian blood transfusion unit caught journalists' imaginations, and many stories were written about it. Indeed, Bethune went out of his way to supply reporters with material to write about.

Up till then, transfusions had normally been performed from one person directly to another, and the creation of a blood bank with blood stored in bottles until needed was still in its pioneering stages. Bethune was really learning as he went.

The unit broadcast over the radio that they were looking for donors. They had to make very tough decisions. Syphilis and malaria were endemic in Spain, and in normal circumstances, every donor should have been tested for both diseases. The unit did not have the means to do this, so they decided that, rather than die, a man would prefer to be saved even if it meant receiving a dose of syphilis, which might be cured later. During the first few weeks, they did no testing except for blood type, although they checked the donors for good health. On opening day there were hundreds of people lining up to give their blood, and Bethune and Sise realized they were in business in a big way.

After a month or so they were performing transfusions all day and collecting blood to leave at hospitals. With a curious kind of fascist efficiency, Madrid was being bombed promptly at four o'clock every afternoon, which left everyone feeling they were living on the edge, even if that precipice was predictable. The unit tried to do person-to-person transfusion as much as possible, because it was safe and added to the "life-giving" atmosphere. What Bethune realized was that people (and they eventually numbered in the thousands) wanted to give their blood as a physical act of belief in the Republic. They were literally giving lifeblood to the cause of democracy.

At Christmastime, Bethune felt the unit had to go up to the front to convince the Spanish doctors to use their service. They went to the Guadarrama, a beautiful range of mountains forming a backdrop to Madrid. They were experimenting and improvising as they went along with the size of containers for the blood, the diameter of their necks, and the amount of sodium nitrate that should be added. Bethune and the others decided that they would accept only a militia man's pay, the equivalent of ten cents a day.

Through the Canadian Committee to Aid Spanish Democracy, Canadians gave thousands of dollars to Bethune's transfusion unit, and the unit served to advertise the cause of a Republican Spain to those who wanted to fight. Bethune's greatest contribution to the development of transfusion was to make real the idea that it was possible to have a large-scale system for the collection and distribution of blood to front-line hospitals and casualty-clearing stations close to the front line. He realized the importance of prompt transfusion, anticipating something that trauma surgeons recognize today as the "golden hour" of opportunity for resuscitation after injury. It's hard to know how many people were saved in the seven months that the transfusion service operated—day and night. But when Bethune left Madrid his program was credited with having achieved a drastic reduction in fatalities among the wounded. One observer estimated that as a result of the Servicio Canadiense de Transfusión de Sangre, 30 percent fewer people were dying. The technique developed by Bethune in Spain has been developed and used in every war since.

Reading over all the accounts of his work, it is startling to see that Bethune's contemporaries in transfusion didn't talk about his contribution. A review of twentieth-century histories of transfusion turns up no references to Bethune, although the Spanish and their contributions receive credit. Bethune's legacy in the blood transfusion service was at least acknowledged by one of the leading historians of the Spanish Civil War, Hugh Thomas, who said that "the medical assistance to the Republic brought many advances of military and civilian surgery and general therapy. Of these, the most outstanding were the remarkable developments in the technique of blood transfusion inspired by the Canadian Dr. Norman Bethune." Perhaps it was Bethune's personality which made many people want to write him out. Certainly in Spain he was abrasive, impatient, and domineering.

By March 1937, Bethune wanted to assume authority over the distribution of blood for transfusion along the whole of the six-hundred-mile front. But the opposite happened: the unit realized they were going to be transferred over to the Republican army's medical corps because of the violent confrontations—which were just short of fisticuffs— they had had with some of their Spanish counterparts, whose xenophobia seemed to be aggravated by Bethune's pronounced self-assurance and heedless courage. The Servicio Canadiense de Transfusión de Sangre lost its autonomy after only four months of activity and was formally transferred to the jurisdiction of the Spanish medical corps. Bethune was made an honorary *comandante*, Sise was an honorary captain, and they wore distinguishing badges to that effect. Bethune insisted that the ranks be strictly honorary, because the Canadian Foreign Enlistment Act of 1937 would have made them all liable to prosecution when they returned to Canada if it was thought they had enlisted. Under the act, which was aimed at the Canadian volunteers of the Mackenzie-Papineau Battalion, it was an offence "to enlist with a foreign state at war with a friendly state" and "to leave or intend to leave Canada to enlist," which could lead to imprisonment for two years. The service was renamed the Instituto Hispano-Canadiense de Transfusión de Sangre. "We had lost our nationalistic opportunity," noted Sise, "but the staff was increased to a hundred, the number of donors nearly reached 4000 and there were 5 delivery vehicles in only 5 months."

Bethune's action in Spain, though it didn't last very long, was dramatic, radical, and successful. He knew how to get things done. He acted, but he didn't always understand the consequences of his actions on others. Sise tried "to rein Bethune in because I could see the difficulties too vividly and try and make him do things in a more organized way. But he was always a person who had absolutely no inhibitions, no gap between thought and action. Once he thought about something and decided something was worthwhile doing, he would just go right out and do it and he would leave a trail of annoyed bureaucrats and hurt feelings behind him. I was the guy usually who had to trail on behind and clean up the mess."

As if things weren't complicated enough, Bethune's involvement with a woman named Kasja, who had been suspected of spying for the fascists, made him a suspect figure. Biographer Larry Hannant, and author Michael Petrou in his excellent book *Renegades: Canadians in the Spanish Civil*

War, both examined Bethune's relationship to her. A contemporary report from the Communist International organization in Moscow that has recently been made available suggests that Bethune himself was a spy for the fascists because he was constantly taking note of bridges, distances, locations, and timetables of trains. The fact that this was all essential information for somebody operating an ambulance system in a war-torn country with thousands of fleeing refugees and bomb-strafed roads is not taken into account. The notion of Bethune as a spy entangled in a liaison with Kasja, who by all accounts fitted the stereotype of the gorgeous Valkyrie of Nordic myth (complete with flowing red-gold hair), feeds the image of Bethune as lady-killer and mystery man. Indeed, a fascinating novel by Dennis Bock, *The Communist's Daughter,* uses this relationship as part of a story that draws the Bethune myth down a road that has not been previously travelled.

Bethune realized that the Spanish struggle could be told graphically on film, so he organized and wrote an hour-long documentary, employing the skills of a young Hungarian actor, Charles Korvin. As propaganda, *Heart of Spain* has gripping images. It shows a third of Madrid in ruins, small children giving workers' salutes, training to fight in empty lots, building barricades, and at the same time being children, playing and skipping rope. Overheated lines—"even the olives are bleeding now"—are counterweighted with the vivid and more accurate acknowledgment that "every foot of earth costs blood." There are images of Bethune dealing with the wounded, and his every gesture, though decisive, is filled with a kind of magical tenderness.

Sise felt that Bethune was very run down after this enormous burst of energy over very little time, and that he was tiring out because he had only one functioning lung. He remembers Bethune suddenly having to almost collapse onto a sofa and pull a rug over himself to recharge his batteries for an hour or two.

The unit all worked to the point of exhaustion, leaving from Barcelona, say, at three in the morning and driving 340 miles south to Toledo, moving along the front lines distributing blood to troops, and looping back to Barcelona to refill with supplies. They were sometimes on the road for twenty-four hours without a break. In this mix of total physical fatigue and high tension, there was constant conflict with the Spanish transfusion unit. And according to his colleagues, Bethune was drinking heavily.

But with a relatively small amount of money and a tiny group on the front, Bethune changed how the wounded could be treated, and he brought to the Republican side a sense of innovative commitment that must have helped boost morale. The enthusiasm was infectious. The unit made short-wave radio broadcasts to audiences in North America, some of which were heard in Canada through a little station called Estacion U.G.T. To make the transmissions, they would slip out in the dark and pick their way through the moonlit streets of Madrid using a password. These sorties had a fairy-tale quality. They would go to a cellar off the Gran Via with mattresses against the windows, where they'd speak into microphones wondering whether anybody could possibly be listening. Once, miraculously, Sise's mother heard them in her home in Westmount, Quebec.

Bethune was attempting to broadcast to the world the meaning of the struggle in Spain, and his scripts, which were also published, show that he was an effective propagandist.

To Spaniards on Christmas Eve 1936, he broadcast:

> Comrades of Spain, I and my comrades of the Blood Transfusion Service have the honour to be in Spain as the representatives of the Canadian Committee to Aid Spanish Democracy.
>
> ... [Headquartered in Toronto, Canada] workers and intellectuals, liberals and socialists and communists ... join hands with the United States

of Spain—the International Anti-Fascists of the old and new worlds.

What Spain does today ... will decide the future of the world for the next hundred years. If you are defeated, the world will fall back into the new Dark Ages of Fascism—if you are successful as we are confident you will be successful, we will go forward into the glories of the golden age of economic and political democracy....

Remember we Canadian workers are with you. We have come here as into the opening battle of the world revolution.... Ask how we can help you. You will find us ready. Your fight is our fight. Your victory is our victory....

What is needed in Spain:

1. More physicians who speak French or German, if not Spanish.
2. More brain surgeons, on account of the high proportion of head injuries owing to lack of proper protection of the skull by steel helmets.
3. More foreign nurses to be attached to hospitals treating the wounded from the International Brigade.

4. A convalescent home or club for ... members of the international brigade. Think of being discharged and wandering about Madrid, lonely, discouraged and sad.

5. We need more ambulances, more splints, more X-ray films.

On January 1, 1937, he was on the air again:

There has been very heavy fighting today ... the bursts of field gun-fire has been almost continuous, reminding [me] of the barrages on the Western Front of 1915. To these dangers are added the attacks of Fascist bombers, attended by their fighting escort.

Within sight of these planes is a cemetery of the International Brigade. Here ... lie the bodies of those men who died to save Spain and dedicated their young lives to the cause of Spanish democracy.

These young men volunteered fully and they traveled, many in disguise, thousands of miles from their native lands working their way out secretly to escape police terrorism ... facing overwhelming odds of trained mercenary professional troops, against a military machine dominated by German and Italian Staff Officers, fighting with rifles some of them dating before 1914 against modern German and Italian machine guns without steel helmets or proper clothing.

Bethune went to great lengths in his vivid descriptions to emphasize that the battle lines were clearly drawn between right and wrong, between the oppression by the fascists and the liberation of the Republicans.

On January 2, 1937:

Madrid is paradoxically enough the most peaceful city in Europe.

It is a city at equilibrium within itself, a city without the intense class antagonisms and discords that are called disorder in any other city. That is due to its homogenous society—the workers, the small shopkeepers and petit-bourgeois all molded into one class with one idea—winning the war against the fascist aggressor.... No police are needed to maintain the law. Every member, every citizen is under the strict necessity of order—

self-imposed and conscious. [It must be remembered that Madrid was under a two-and-a-half-year siege and Bethune is trying to boost Republican morale and paint a picture of a socialist utopia prevailing under extreme conditions.] Private property is respected. On large magnificent mansions which once belonged to the late so-called nobility, one sees signs such as: "citizens this property belongs to you. Respect it." Note the wording of the sign—not "belongs to the state"— the state is an institution superior to and above the people but—"belongs to you." So if you or I damage it we are damaging our own property.

We were heavily bombed from the air today about 12 noon. 12 huge Italian tri-motored bombers came over the city and bombed not only positions of military importance, but a poor quarter of the city called Cuatro Caminos. This is a district some miles behind the front-lines inhabited by the poorest people living in one or two-storey mud and brick dwellings. The massacred victims were mainly women, children and old people....

What is the object of these bombings of lowly civilian habitations? Is it to produce panic in the city? Because if so, it is a completely cruel useless and wanton endeavour. These people cannot be terrified.

In the first week of February 1937, the transfusion unit made an enormous journey of some 370 miles toward Almería along the Mediterranean coast. Franco's combined forces had launched an assault on the southern city of Málaga and the city's defences were smashed. When twenty-five thousand German, Italian, and Moorish troops entered the town, over a hundred thousand civilian refugees took to the roads north toward Almería. Bethune wrote a pamphlet, "The Crime on the Road: Malaga–Almeria," in which he described the hideous situation they encountered head-on:

Now imagine 150,000 men, women and children setting out for safety to the town situated over two hundred kilometres away. There is only one road they can take. There is no other way of escape…. The journey women, children and old people must face will take five days and five nights at least. There will be no food to be found in the villages, no trains, no buses to transport them…. The Fascists bomb them from the air and fired at them from the ships at sea ... the largest, most terrible evacuation of the city in modern times.... We set out at six o'clock in the evening along the Malaga road.... Here were the strong with all their goods on donkeys, mules and horses ... we counted five thousand [children] under 10 years of age and at least one thousand of them barefoot and many of them clad only in a single garment. They were slung over their mothers' shoulders or clung to their hands. Here a father staggered along with two children of one and two years of age on his back.... At 88 kilometres from Almeria they beseeched us to go no farther, that the Fascists were just behind. By this time we had passed so many distressed women and children that we thought it best to turn back and start transporting the worst cases to safety.

It was difficult to choose which to take. Our car was beseeched by a mob of frantic mothers and fathers who with tired outstretched arms held up to us their children, their eyes and faces swollen and congested after four days of sun and dust....

Children with blood-stained rags wrapped around their arms and legs, children without

THOSE WHO IN THEIR LIVES FOUGHT FOR LIFE

shoes, their feet swollen to twice their size, crying helplessly from pain, hunger and fatigue.... Children crying out the names of their separated relatives lost in the mob. How could we choose between taking a child dying of dysentery or a mother silently watching us with great sunken eyes carrying against her open breast her child born on the road two days ago. She had stopped walking for ten hours only.... Many old people simply gave up the struggle, lay down by the side of the road and waited for death.... We first decided to take only children and mothers, then the separation between father and child, husband and wife became too cruel.

The second night they were in Almería, Sise drove in with a load of families and brought them to a kind of sanatorium on the outskirts, but the Spanish people in charge seemed in no hurry to produce anything like food or drink. Bethune suddenly became enraged and

did one of his usual stunts. He went charging into the kitchen, not knowing any Spanish, except a few words, and he just ordered people around and grabbed huge saucepans, put them on the stove, grabbed all the milk and bread he could find and heated them together, cursing everybody at the same time, ordering them to get moving, all in a furious tone. The poor Spaniards were very upset and taken aback because they'd not been conscious of any dereliction of duty, they were just following the normal pace. We fed those kids … and put them to bed, and when I woke up in the morning the transformation was incredible. The kids were completely revived and as lively as crickets; they were rushing around playing, full of energy. That was the sort of thing [Bethune] did. And of course when he operated like that with people at the higher army level he made lots of enemies. A lot of people were very resentful.

Almería, now filled with forty thousand refugees, was heavily bombed by German and Italian airplanes. Bethune picked up the bodies of three dead children from the pavement, where they had been waiting to receive bread and milk, the only food some of them had had for days. In "The Crime on the Road" he described the shrieks of the bereaved mothers, the moans of wounded children, and the curses of men. The only crime these unarmed citizens had committed, he concluded, was having voted to elect a government of the people committed to the "most moderate alleviation of a crushing burden of centuries of the greed of capitalism."

Sleep-deprived, nerves on edge, temper continually enflamed, Bethune was on the verge of a complete breakdown. His Canadian friends Ted Allan, Hazen Sise, and Henning Sorensen were aware of this; they wanted to protect him, basically from himself. It would be best, they felt, if he left Spain. We will never know how he was persuaded to leave, but we sense the depths of his desperation in an "Apology for Not Writing Letters." It was to all of his friends who had wondered

> why I, who think of you so often with love and affection, have not written—or so briefly—since my arrival in Spain.
>
> I had thought to say simply … I am a man of action; I have no time to write. Yet as I look at those words, I see they are false. They simply are not true. In fact, I have had plenty of time to write you, that is if I cared to write, but in truth, I did not care.… Why have I not written to those of you who I know without illusion would like to hear

from me? Why is it I cannot put down one word after another on paper and make a letter out of them?...

First of all, I don't feel like writing. I don't feel the necessity of communication. I don't feel strongly the necessity of a reconstruction of experience—my actions and the actions of others—into the form of art which a letter should take.... At present I don't feel any necessity to communicate these experiences. They are in me, they have changed me, but I don't want to talk about them. I don't want to talk about them yet.

Besides, I am afraid to write to you. I am afraid of the banality of words, of the vocal, the verbal, of the literary reconstruction. I'm afraid they won't be true.

To share with you what I have seen, what I have experienced in the past six months is impossible without art. Without art experience becomes on the one hand, the diluted bare-bones of fact—a static still life ... on the other hand, the swollen exaggerated shapes of fantastically-coloured romanticism. Yes, I could write but I am ashamed to write—like this: 'we were heavily shelled today.

It was very uncomfortable. Fifty people were killed
in the streets. The weather is lovely now, although
the winter has been hard. I am well. I think of you
often. Yes, it is true, I love you. Goodbye.'

I put them down and look at these words with
horror and disgust. I wish I could describe to you
how much I dislike these words 'uncomfortable'.
Good God! What a word to describe the paralyz-
ing fear that seizes one when a shell bursts with a
great roar and crash nearby; 'killed' for these poor
huddled bodies of rags and blood lying in such
strange shapes face down on the cobblestones or
with sightless eyes upturned to a cruel and indif-
ferent sky; 'lovely' when the sun falls on our
numbed faces like a benediction; 'well' when to be
alive is well enough; 'think' for that cry rising from
our hearts day by day for remembered ones; 'love'
for this ache of separation. So you see it's no good.

He goes on to try out several theories of art and reflects
on the role of the subconscious mind.

Most great artists of this world have been—thank
heaven—stupid in the worldly sense. They didn't

think too much. They simply painted. Driven on by an irresistible internal compulsion they painted as they did, as they must paint....

The artist needs among other things leisure, immense quietness, privacy, and aloneness. The environment in which he has his being are those dark, sunless, yet strangely illuminated depths of the world's subconscious—the warm, pulsating, yet quiet depths of the other world.

He comes up into the light of every day, like a great leviathan of the deep, breaking the smooth surface of accepted things gay, serious, sportive, and destructive. In the bright banal glare of day, he enjoys the purification of violence, the catharsis of action. His appetite for life is enormous. He enters eagerly into the life of man, of all men. He becomes all men in himself.

... The function of the artist is to disturb. His duty is to arouse the sleeper to shake the complacent pillars of the world. He reminds the world of its dark ancestry, shows the world its present, and points the way to its new birth.... In a world terrified of change, he preaches revolution—the principle of life. He is an agitator, a disturber of the

peace—quick, impatient, positive, restless and disquieting. He is the creative spirit of life working in
the soul of men.

Bethune's sense of the artist as someone who breaks down
all barriers is consistent with his work as a surgeon and as a
social activist. For him, disease and poverty were not simply
conditions of human life but enemies of the kind of life that
he felt human beings must have. In that letter from Spain,
he aligns himself as a mental revolutionary, but in fact everything he did was a guerrilla action using methods of irregular warfare. When he could be his own master and create
around himself an area of action in which he knew he had
both competence and expertise, he was at his very best. Any
obstacle to that kind of action was enormously frustrating to
him and caused him to behave badly.

In April 1937, he wrote to the Spanish transfusion unit
that his "function as chief of the organization … has come
to a natural end." What he had accomplished in a mere
seven months in Spain was astonishing. He had virtually
invented a method of storing and transporting blood to
where it was needed; a method that predated the establishment of the first blood bank unit in the United States, at
Cook County Hospital, Chicago, by almost one year. Now

he was going home to Canada to raise money and awareness for the cause of Republican Spain.

No one tells us how Bethune got out of Spain, but when he arrived back in New York by ship on June 7, 1937, he gave an interview to the Montreal *Gazette*, in which he asked, "What's the matter with England, France, the United States, Canada? Are they afraid that by supplying arms to the Loyalist [Republican] forces they'll start a World War? Why, the world war has started. In fact, it's in its third stage—Manchuria, Ethiopia, and now Spain. It's democracy against Fascism." The journalist described Bethune as "flushed; his lean body quivered [as] he pounded his fist in emphasis [and] fairly shouted the words." In the interview, Bethune described his work in Spain with the small Canadian unit and his presence at the retreat from Málaga. He mentioned that he attended services at the Lutheran church in Madrid every Sunday and that all the churches were open (much of the propaganda on the fascist side referred to the purported atheism of the Republican Loyalists, including the raping of nuns and the destruction of churches).

His adventure in Spain and now his return home to raise money and support was organized by the Canadian Committee to Aid Spanish Democracy, which made a concerted effort not to be labelled as Red so that it could gather into its fold as many people from the centre to the far left as possible. Now that Bethune was back they urged him not to emphasize the fact that he was a Communist.

His first speaking engagement was in Toronto on June 14. A parade almost half a mile long formed at Union Station and marched north on University Avenue to the front lawn of the Ontario legislature buildings at Queen's Park. The assembled crowd numbered some five thousand people, and it was just after Bethune's speech that he was asked for the first time since returning from Spain whether he was a Communist. He replied, "Look here, let's get this thing straight. You can call me a Socialist if you like. I am a Socialist in the same way that millions of sane people are Socialists. I want to see people getting a square deal and I hate Fascism. The clenched fist is used as the People's Front salute. It's used in Spain by everybody who is against the Fascists. That's really all it means—anti-Fascism. Why, Premier Blum, of France, uses it and he's no Communist. I should describe it as a reply to the raised hand salute of the Fascist." There is a photograph of him in the *Toronto Star* surrounded by huge crowds, including nurses carrying a banner reading "Welcome to Doctor Bethune" and "Youth Supports Spanish Democracy."

This excitement of rallying thousands to the cause perhaps helped make up for having to leave Spain, which must have been a crushing disappointment for Bethune. One of the people who knew him before he went to Spain felt that the man who returned had lost his "sparkle" and noted that "he didn't laugh the way he used to. The spring in his step was gone.... He was drinking heavily." It must have been very difficult to come down from the heady excitement of the previous months. Some of the places where he was now promoting the cause, such as Kirkland Lake or Prince Albert, could not have felt more remote from the fires that would soon be consuming the rest of the world. And yet his speeches, in Hannant's estimation, inspired Canadian "volunteers to join the Mackenzie-Papineau Battalion and fight in Spain."

Whether he was denying or asserting his Communist sympathies, he always made the point that there was no hope for peace until people realized that the causes of war were economic and that it was the struggle for international justice that lay at the heart of the great conflagration now building.

On July 20, he was honoured at a banquet in the St. Charles Hotel in Winnipeg and declared publicly for the first time: "I have the honour to be a Communist.... They call me a Red because I saved five hundred lives." He angrily told his audience that when he asked that his blood service be officially recognized by the Canadian government so they could get their equipment through France from England without having to pay customs duty, he was refused. "Ottawa said we were too radical. I don't think my method of saving lives could be considered too radical." He almost always concluded these addresses with a complete condemnation of England's policy in international affairs, its lack of support for the legally elected government of Spain and the Republican cause, and a plea to all progressive political parties to fight fascism. He raised $1,500 at that one banquet—$43,000 in today's money.

His audiences were hugely enthusiastic and interrupted frequently with applause. He spoke to nine thousand people in Mount Royal Arena in Montreal on June 18; the audience gave $3,000 to the cause. The tour was an unqualified success.

Bethune continued to state that profit must be taken away from the practice of medicine because a doctor's knowledge must be available to all people, even those who could not buy it.

> The health of the people of a country is that country's principal asset. In my practice I hated the

two, five and ten dollar bills that came between me and my patients. Many other doctors feel the same way. I believe that doctors should be civil servants and that treatment should be free to the public and paid for out of general taxation.

As his declarations became more overtly political, it must have become obvious to Bethune that he would have to find another cause into which he could throw himself.

As Michael Petrou points out in *Renegades*, those who, like Bethune, saw the interference of the fascist powers in Spain as a prelude to a larger war were certainly right. Countries such as Canada, Great Britain, and the United States wanted to stay out of it because they did not want to be seen to be supporting leftist causes, even though the left had legally gained power in Spain in a free and democratic election. Bethune's experience in seeing first-hand the kind of warfare that was waged against civilians by the massive airpower of the Germans on behalf of Franco left him in no doubt that this was not simply a war about one nation's choice of government.

It would take Canada more than sixty years to recognize the legitimacy of the Republican cause and the contribution of Canadians to it. But Norman Bethune will be remembered among "The names of those who in their lives fought for life / Who wore at their heart's core the fire's centre. / Born of the sun, they travelled a short while towards the sun, / And left the vivid air signed with their honour." The great English poet Stephen Spender wrote those words. According to Hazen Sise, Spender and Bethune met once, in Madrid.

CHAPTER EIGHT

Every Leader Starts by First Leading Himself

Why China? What caused Bethune to end his hugely successful speaking tour of North America raising funds for the Canadian Committee to Aid Spanish Democracy? He felt at first that he wouldn't be very good at giving these speeches, but as the tour went on, he drew thousands of people and proved to be a riveting speaker. It must have flattered his ego and his profound sense of what he was as a person that he could engage huge audiences and tell them what he believed: that fascism must be defeated at all costs.

But Bethune was not good in supporting roles. He needed to turn the spotlight on himself because he sincerely believed that was where he belonged. Rather than raising money for the cause, he needed to be the person implementing the cause.

At the beginning of July 1937, he began to sense what that cause should be. The Japanese had launched a full-scale attack against China's major cities, and the Canadian newspapers were filled with it. Canada felt benevolent toward China. There were still relatively large numbers of Canadian missionaries even in the remotest parts of China, and churchgoing Canadians must have heard many a sermon encouraging them to fill rice bowls and save little girls from bound feet and prostitution. After conquering Manchuria and installing the puppet emperor in 1931, the Japanese were ready to continue conquering the rest of China. The Chinese appeal to the League of Nations to take action against Japan was not acted upon, and the Japanese undoubtedly felt emboldened.

It didn't help that China itself was torn by civil war between the Nationalist Kuomintang government of Chiang Kai-shek (quartered in Nanjing in the southeast) and the Chinese Communists under the leadership of Mao Zedong, which had just completed the Long March to the northwest. Initially, Chiang Kai-shek had been bested by the extraordinary Communist general Zhu De, but Chiang struck back with an army of four hundred thousand, encircling the Communists and killing or starving to death a million peasants. About one hundred thousand men, women, and children were forced into a circuitous retreat that took them from Jiangxi west to Yan'an, in the mountains of Shanxi Province. This is one of the most extraordinary marches in military history; Napoleon's retreat from Moscow pales in comparison. Beginning in 1934, they crossed eighteen mountain chains and twenty-four large rivers, zigzagging south and west, then swinging far to the north, traversing the entire breadth of China. They crossed six territories of Aboriginal tribespeople and took sixty-two cities. The first six thousand soldiers arrived in Yan'an under the leadership of Mao more than a year later, in October 1935. They had fought their way over six thousand miles. Another fourteen thousand followed in different battalions. Eighty thousand had perished on the way.

In December 1936, the head of the Nationalists, Chiang Kai-shek, flew to Xian (now known for the famous terra-cotta army since uncovered there) in order to organize a concentrated attack on the Red Army by two of his northern generals. But instead, the Nationalist generals kidnapped Chiang and forced him to form a patriotic United Front with the Communists in order to throw back the Japanese invasion. Learning of China's decision to unify its forces, the Japanese attacked on July 7, 1937.

At that moment, Bethune was speaking in Rouyn-Noranda, Quebec, coincidentally the place where he had once thought he might take up a position as a young doctor. Several months later he told an audience in Salmon Arm,

B.C., that China was going to be his next stop. One wonders how the audience reacted to this man who had returned from Spain and was raising money for the Spanish cause when he announced he was now planning to go to China.

The Canadian Communist leader, Tim Buck, got Bethune the support of the Communist Party of the United States of America, the China League Council, and the American League for Peace and Democracy. In early January 1938, Bethune left Vancouver for Hong Kong on the SS *Empress of Asia*. He was accompanied by an American surgeon, Dr. Charles Parsons, and a Canadian nurse, Jean Ewen.

Ewen had been working in Canada after spending five years in China as a midwife-paramedic and spoke fluent Chinese. She is completely left out of Ted Allan's 1952 account of Bethune, *The Scalpel, The Sword*—as if she had never existed. Forty years later, Ewen wrote her own book, and in it she gives a vivid, down-to-earth description of her long journey to get to Yan'an with Bethune and Parsons. When Ewen told her story, she noted, "I do not attempt to judge.... No innuendo is intended, although I am sure there are those who shout liar, prevaricator, Trotskyite, or whatever. Should you wish to verify the events be my guest. An enterprising individual with a knack for diligent search will find them to be true." Ewen's father, Tom—a Communist who, she writes, was more interested in socialism than in being a father—was arrested for sedition in 1931 and spent five years in the federal penitentiary in Kingston. In 1933 she took off alone for China, mainly working as a midwife in Shandong and north of the Yellow River. She delivered babies and she learned about the local customs, such as saving the placenta, drying it, and grinding it up for medicine. Her experiences brought her very close to the Chinese people, and she was not judgmental about their practices. She returned to Canada in June 1937 not knowing that she would soon be back under very different conditions. Working at St. Joseph's Hospital in Toronto, she was still thinking about China when she was summoned one day to Communist Party headquarters on King Street. She was told about Dr. Norman Bethune, the surgeon who had just come back from Spain, where he had organized blood transfusion units. She said she had heard a lot about Bethune but not much of it was good. Sam Carr, who was in charge of the headquarters, said, "I want you to go and look after him," and she said she would.

They were an unlikely threesome—Norman Bethune, the feisty Jean Ewen, and the alcoholic Dr. Parsons. Bethune wanted to get rid of Parsons as soon as they landed in Shanghai because he was drunk all the time, but Ewen felt he should stay. At the next stop, in Hong Kong, Parsons admitted he had spent much of their expense money on booze. "Dr. Bethune was furious," wrote Ewen. "I had not seen such a temper before, except in my father. He stomped and kicked everything in sight except Parsons." Parsons would not be accompanying them any farther.

They had gone to China to offer themselves as medical help in the same spirit in which Bethune had gone to Spain; he was simply a doctor joining the United Front, the coalition of Nationalists and Communists fighting the Japanese, and hoping to be helpful. On January 30, 1938, they were greeted in Hangzhou by Zhou Enlai (Chou En-lai), who was both a Communist leader and minister of war in the United Front government, and by Chin Bo Qu, the coordinator of medical services of the Eighth Route Army. They had no difficulty communicating because both of the Chinese spoke fluent English. "Mr. Chou was under the impression that Canada was wild bush country inhabited by Indians, a sprinkling of Frenchmen, and the Dionne quintuplets," wrote Ewen. "When they found I was fluent in Chinese, they did not speak English to me anymore. Mr. Chou was a very dashing fellow even by Western standards. His charisma, combined with the fact that he was multi-lingual, put him at ease in any company. He was usually the centre of the gathering. His eyes were usually very soft and inquiring, with an amused twinkle, but they could also be very severe."

The group was asked by Dr. Lim, the head of the Chinese Red Cross, whether they would be willing to join the Eighth Route Army, then in the northwest, in the Chin-Ch'a-Chi border region in the mountains of Shanxi Province, two hundred miles from Yan'an and three hundred from Xian. Lim wanted to have a coordinated system of hospitals with an ambulance corps to transport the seriously wounded to the hospitals at the rear. According to Jean Ewen: "Dr. Bethune turned to me and asked if I would go with him. I said sure.... Chou En-lai welcomed us to the 8th Route Army Medical Service and said he couldn't offer us anything but hard work and Dr. Bethune could expect nothing but a host of grateful patients."

They were to go with a unit that had, of all things, an obstetrical team. This made sense once they learned that the Eighth Route Army also looked after all medical services for the entire civilian population in their areas. Their journey of six weeks to Yan'an was a strenuous zigzag route by foot and rail; they waited at stations for trains that would take them more or less in the right direction and they dodged Japanese bombs and bullets. They left Hangzhou by third-class train, joining refugees, and made their way to Zhengzhou in

Henan Province. Having missed their connection for Xian, they spent the night on the floor of a freight shed at the end of the platform with a woman and her baby, whom Bethune was able to spoon feed with some dried milk reconstituted with boiling water. The woman had no money and Bethune gave her some, which she accepted reluctantly and with tears because she felt humiliated. To help her save face, Bethune told her that it was not charity: when the war was over he would come back for repayment. As soon as they reached Dong Guan, Bethune started operating, setting shoulders, removing bullets, and performing an amputation on a leg that was gangrenous.

At the beginning of the long and dangerous journey to Yan'an, Bethune had told Ewen what he expected of her.

> [He] took this opportunity to have a little talk on just what he expected of me. I was never to call him by his first name, a sin I had not yet committed. Ours was to be a doctor-nurse relationship, otherwise we were to have no particular contact. I told him not to worry. It could be no other way in professional work. Then, too, I was not to take it upon myself to diagnose or treat patients. He knew I had not but he was just telling me. I wondered what

brought that on and I was hopping mad. I was a servant, no more, no less. I did not show my anger, at least I hope I didn't. I resolved to put forward every effort to please the good doctor.

Partway north, they had to get off their train and ford the freezing Yellow River, in which chunks of ice were still floating, and then walk with their baggage to a train station about a mile away, where they were to catch whatever transport happened to come along. They found an empty boxcar at the end of a train with two bales of hay in it, which they used to make warm mattresses for their bedrolls. Some young teachers heading toward the new Academy of National Resistance in Wutai Shan joined them. The train being late to depart, they entertained one another, Bethune playing the ukulele he had brought along and singing Spanish songs. This improvised travel continued on the 370 miles to Yan'an. Two days after leaving Dong Guan they reached the China Inland Mission, only ten miles away from the advancing Japanese. Ewen talks about Bethune's frustration because he could not treat the wounded; their railway car was shunted off to another train and she was sure he would blame her for it, which he promptly did. He held her personally responsible: "Of all the damned inefficiency I have ever seen … (swear words) Where in hell are your brains?" Trains full of old people, children, and the wounded, all refugees, passed them. At Won Woon they stopped to rest under a tree. They were both leaning against it when they noticed little drops coming down on them. To their horror they saw that up in the branches was the rotting body of a young child: "'My God, my God,' whispered Bethune." Ewen didn't know whether it was a curse, a requiem, or a prayer.

Every place they stopped, their little group, which included several servants and an interpreter, was approached for medical help. Bethune was, says Ewen, "like the Good Samaritan [binding] the wounds of all who came to him." Once, with forty cars on one train, they became a very visible target and were badly bombed. Bethune looked after the wounded as best he could, but Ewen felt she could hardly function she was so afraid. "Dr. Bethune didn't get angry," she said, "but he pontificated: 'Every man must have two baptisms in his life—once with water and once with fire. You have just had your baptism of fire.' 'You are nothing but a bloody missionary,' I said, without thinking." Bethune flew into a rage. "He yelled and screamed, talking so quickly that I don't think he knew exactly what he was saying. 'Don't you ever say anything like that again, you dizzy bitch!'"

Later, under the stress of disagreements about how to treat certain patients, Ewen felt that although Bethune was

> a dedicated humanitarian ... even dedicated peo-
> ple didn't have all the answers. He said nothing
> until after we had something to eat. Then he sug-
> gested that I take a walk with him. I knew by the
> air of professional dignity he assumed that anger
> was about to explode. "You are truculent, self-
> sufficient, overconfident and absolutely no use to
> me—and you are also a disgrace to your illustrious
> father," he fumed. I agreed with him. I always
> tried to be a disgrace to my father.
>
> At this point I felt I was just about the last per-
> son in creation who should have made this jour-
> ney with him. "I will be pleased to leave this
> bloody unit when we reach Xi'an," I told him.

More and more soldiers were coming in, their wounds infected, and they found themselves in a no-man's land on the Fen River in southwest Shanxi Province, still a hundred miles from Xian and ahead of the advancing Japanese army by only a few miles. They were at the rear of a retreating Chinese army. "I was sure now that I was the last person on earth who should have come with this man," wrote Ewen. "He felt there was something missing in my make-up.... In his work with the sick and wounded, he was a man dedicated to the service of all mankind.... Compassion for suffering humanity he had in abundance and would go out of his way to help a patient as I have not seen many doctors do."

One night Bethune talked to Ewen about his wife, Frances, calling her "the light of his life." This was the Bethune who could be sloppily emotional, elaborating on how wonderful Frances was and how he was entirely responsible for the failure of their marriage. "He was very unhappy in his personal life and couldn't make the adjustments required for lasting relationships. He did not accept himself or his own limitations. Was proud to a fault, and his irascibility touched with arrogance made him untouchable."

On his birthday, March 4, Bethune noted that just one year earlier he had been in Madrid. On this, his forty-eighth birthday, he dressed six wounded soldiers, noting that they had "nothing but neglected minor injuries—all others have died on the way back." The next day they left for another village on the east bank of the Yellow River, a place the Japanese had burned when they passed through two days previously. Bethune recounted the unforgettable sight that met them.

Lit by a dozen fires, five thousand men were collected with trunks, carts, mules, horses, artillery and great piles of stores waiting to cross the river into Chingxi. The light of the fires was reflected back from a steep wall-like mountainside. The river rushes between two high cliffs. The swift current (12 miles an hour) carries great floating ice floes which clash against each other far out on the dark surface. The whole scene is wild and fantastic. Lying on top of rice bags, we finally sleep at midnight. The man next to me has a handgrenade in his belt and as he turns in his sleep, it sticks into my back.

In this region they witnessed a battle and saw machine-gun bullets striking the water a hundred yards away from them. They had to make a dash across a piece of open land, where they were fired on again. They'd heard that the Japanese force pursuing them consisted of about 500 cavalry and several batteries of field guns and infantry—altogether 20,000 men. The next day the Japanese artillery arrived on the opposite bank and shelled them all day for three days. It would take them a month to cover the entire 600 miles; and the last 220 miles to Xian was entirely by foot.

When they met Zhu De, Mao's representative in Xian, on March 22, 1938, they were told that all of them were thought to have been killed. Canada had even been notified. They were given the March 12 edition of the *Chicago Tribune*. In it was an article that said they were dead, with a picture of Bethune. After the meeting, they prepared to go north by truck, first 125 miles to Yan'an and then across the Yellow River to the Wutai mountains, where the partisans and the Eighth Route Army were beleaguered. Somehow, in spite of axel-bending roads, they made their way to Yan'an in less than a week.

At eleven o'clock on the very night they arrived in Yan'an, they were summoned to meet Mao Zedong. Bethune was already in bed, but it took him only two minutes to get dressed. As he passed Ewen, he said to her, "You don't need to go." But she reports that

> in a very short sarcastic manner, I assured him "since I have not been officially expelled from this so-called medical unit, I think I'm entitled to go and be represented!" The good doctor assured me he had not meant it in the way I understood it. And so I went to see the chairman of the Communist Party of China, even though I had no credentials to present.

Ewen's account of this meeting is immediate and fresh.

The messenger who escorted us to Chairman Mao's quarters explained that the chairman worked during the night hours, from midnight to sometimes eight or nine in the morning when it was quiet, and that he did not usually see people unless they were important.... The guard outside Mao's house pushed back the heavy padded drape (there was no door) which covered the entrance. We stepped into an almost dark cavern.... [Her memory was incorrect. It was the entrance to the local rice merchant's house.]

A man stood at the table with one hand resting on a book near its edge, his face turned to the door. He wore a blue cotton uniform like any other soldier in Yanan, but his cap was a peaked cap with the red, five-pointed star on it. His shadow on the wall seemed to accentuate his height. The flickering shadows on the walls lent a strange quality to the scene, a murkiness broken only by the glow of the candle.

The man came towards us smiling, and in a rather high pitched voice said, "Welcome,

welcome." He held his hands out to Dr. Bethune, who accepted his greetings in a like manner. The Chinese leader's hands were long and sensitive, soft as a woman's. Without speaking, the two men just stared at each other for a moment, then they embraced like brothers. The Chairman's face was crowned with a high forehead and a shock of very thick unruly black hair. His sensual mouth flashed into a beaming smile as he sat down at the table where he had been working with his secretary. The secretary could speak fluent English so I was relieved of my duty. Chairman Mao spoke no language but Chinese.… After small talk about the weather, Dr. Bethune presented his credentials from the Communist Party of Canada. His card was printed on a square of white silk, signed by Tim Buck, secretary of the party and adorned by the Party's seal. Chairman Mao took the credentials with great ceremony, bordering on reverence and said, "We shall transfer you to the Communist Party of China so that you will be an inalienable part of this country now." At this point all he asked of me was where I had learned to speak such good Chinese.

Mao told them how much the partisans were in need of good medical care in the Wutai mountains and said that he thought Dr. Bethune would do very well; he was concerned, however, about how the nurse would be able to survive. Then the conversation took a different turn.

> After a time Mao asked me, "Don't you think that Dr. Bethune looks like Lenin?" He stood up where he could look at the Doctor's profile.
>
> "Oh yes, only Dr. Bethune has a better shaped head at the back than Lenin," I chirped brightly.
>
> The secretary told Bethune the gist of our conversation. To say that the doctor was delighted would be to state his feelings mildly. He was flattered. Eventually the four of us got into a discussion of flat heads, and the subject took up a great deal of time without us reaching any reasonable conclusions. The night flew by on wings, and before we knew it, April 2nd had arrived.

That fateful meeting has been recorded in one of the most famous propaganda posters of all time, showing Chairman Mao and Norman Bethune sitting at a table together. They are portrayed as equals, two men deep in earnest conversation, alone, without interpreters, without any distractions. When Bethune met the leaders of the Chinese Communist Party, it was as if water had suddenly found its own level. The man who had condemned his father as a hypocrite, who threw surgical instruments with impatience, treated poor people for free, and taught children art was totally fused with the Chinese purpose. He was welcomed and given the keys to the kingdom, a freedom offered only to the top echelon of the party. The Communists, determined to drive out the Japanese, admired Bethune's pragmatism and concern for the peasants as well as the soldiers. They identified with his desire to innovate and his genius for improvisation. He could do no wrong, and that, for a human being, was a big responsibility.

Bethune had convinced Mao Zedong that he would be most useful in the Chin-Ch'a-Chi border region to the northwest, only three hundred miles to the west of Beijing. While they were getting ready to go, Bethune and Ewen worked at the Yan'an Hospital until the beginning of May. In his letters home, Bethune always described Ewen as a very capable nurse for whom he had a higher regard than he would ever let on. He noticed that she "showed great pluck and fortitude under her first baptism of fire and immediately after the bomber had passed started to dress the wounded and arrange for their transportation to the nearest village a quarter of a mile away, so that by the time I had walked from the head of the line to the rear where the men were wounded, she had already applied dressings to the most serious ones." Even though he shouted at and remonstrated with her in person, he obviously admired her courage and ability to react quickly to an emergency situation.

By the time they left Yan'an, they had been joined by Dr. Richard Brown, a Canadian surgeon from an Anglican mission. Brown had heard of Bethune in Hangzhou and volunteered to join him on his furlough. He brought much-needed medical supplies that Bethune had stored in Hong Kong. Jean Ewen was left behind in Yan'an and subsequently was sent to Xian to pick up more supplies.

At the beginning of May, Bethune and Brown were en route north to the front. They made their way from Yan'an to Jingchuan and on to Sui Teh. The sandy loess soil of the region packed well into hard surfaces, but because the roads were not graded it made the going difficult. Hundreds of caves were dug into the low mountains in clusters, covering about forty valleys and ravines over a distance of about ten miles, often divided by the Yan River. It was barren, eroded land, no good for growing rice, but the caves afforded excellent protection from bomber planes. At this point they met the chief medical officer of the front, who told them that they should go to Pantang, where there were six hundred wounded and no doctors.

Brown and Bethune agreed to clean up there, and the chief medical officer said they would probably be able to proceed from Pantang to the mountainous region of Wutai Shan, which they wanted to do. Bethune very much appreciated Brown, who spoke Chinese fluently, but he was available for only four months. In return, Brown disliked Bethune intensely, later calling him "psychopathic."

Bethune pleaded in letters to the American Committee for them to send more doctors. They were chasing the wounded, travelling by horseback, Bethune on a white horse presented by General Nie Shicheng, the army's commander. By the time they caught up with the Eighth Route Army, they encountered the following situation:

> All have old neglected wounds of the thigh and leg—most of them incurable except by amputation. Three of the 35 are lying naked on straw-covered k'angs [the ceramic beds that are also stoves] with only a single cotton quilt. The others are still in their old unwashed cotton-padded winter, dirty uniforms. They are without exception, all

anemic, underfed, and dehydrated.... They are dying of sepsis. These are the cases we are asked to operate on. They are bad surgical risks.

To a friend, Bethune wrote:

Have you received a single letter I have written? Perhaps not. Perhaps the American Committee has not received any of my letters, cables and appeals. If such is the case, I beg of you and them to forgive the anxious, irritable and angry tone of my letters. Acting on this assumption, I am not sending this letter directly to you to prevent possible interception.... We are happy and content in our work.

Bethune told his correspondents in Yan'an that they needed ten times the amount of even the most elementary equipment—pails, basins, towels, soap. Most of the patients had not had a bath for nine months and their skin was ingrained with dirt. Sheets were needed because all the wounded were lying on dirty straw; bedpans and urinals were non-existent. There were no splints, no bandage rollers, no safety pins, nothing for sterilizing gauze and cotton. Approximately five hundred artificial legs were needed at once.

He added a list of things to make the patients in makeshift hospitals feel happier, such as radios, gramophones and records, books with plenty of illustrations, games foreign or Chinese, hundreds of coloured pictures or posters to hang on walls. He hoped he would be joined by foreign volunteers. He set out in minute detail what personnel coming to China should bring with them, and advised that they all adopt immediately the uniform of the Eighth Route Army, which could be made by tailors in every little town and city. Then he described the kinds of shoes, boots, riding breeches, and sleeping bags they'd need (the latter from Abercrombie and Fitch in New York), ditto for folding camp chairs. He indicated the kind of small tool kits they should carry, the sizes of screwdrivers and saw-chisels, and recommended "one camel-hair blanket each."

In May, he wrote to a friend that he had lost track of Jean Ewen after they had left her in Yan'an. Many years later, Ewen said that she found a telegram from Bethune at Xian, where she had gone for medical supplies, warning her about how terrible the conditions were and advising her not to follow him and Brown. She stayed as head nurse in Yan'an and returned to Canada just before the attack on Pearl Harbor in 1941. Bethune, however, said:

> I don't know what has happened to Jean. On the 20th of April she left for Xi'an to bring back our American equipment, which had arrived there. I asked her to wire and keep in touch with us and return as soon as she could as both Dr. Brown and I were anxious to get away to the front.... Up to the present she has not turned up here and as we have received no letters or telegrams since leaving I don't know where she is.

Later, in a letter to Dr. Ma-Haide in Xian (who was actually an American named George Hatem, from Buffalo, New York, who went to China in the 1930s and remained there all his life), Bethune asked if Ma-Haide had succeeded "in keeping Ewen? I don't need her. I have trained a first-class staff and have a great interpreter." He added a playful postscript: "Come up and see me some time!" That little in-joke between two North Americans probably gave Bethune a bit of pleasure. He was feeling extremely isolated, especially after Dr. Brown had left in the middle of July to try to raise money. Bethune wrote to another friend that

In this great area [Wutai Shan] of thirteen million people, and 150,000 armed troops, I am the only qualified doctor! The Chinese doctors have all beat it. I am at present "cleaning up" the base hospital of 350 wounded and have done 110 operations in 25 days....

Here everything is needed—all drugs, surgical instruments, etc. The nurses are boys of 12 to 17.... There is no malaria here but a lot of syphilis and tuberculosis.... The hospital needs enlarging to 500. This is an 8th Route Army hospital and is very poor. We can buy drugs in Pei-Ping [Beijing]. These cities are held by the Japs but our troops and partisans go in disguised as peasants and smuggle stuff out. If we had a thousand dollars gold we could fix this place up fine.

In the photos the Chinese took of him at this time, you can see him perhaps thirty pounds thinner than the man who gave speeches across North America in 1937. He looks seventy-five. We see him swimming naked, and his body is lean and bony. Where he still has hair, it is white, and his face is hollow-cheeked. Not once does he mention his own condition in his letters, but one can hardly think he was healthy. Chronic dysentery was the reality, and food was in short supply.

Bethune reported regularly to Mao about his activities: fly-control, number of splints made for arms and legs, identification discs, installation for incineration of garbage, construction of a bath house. "About $5000 will be needed in all for the winter," he wrote in one letter to Mao.

In his letters Bethune talks about being isolated and alone, but he was accompanied by several Chinese through his whole time in China. One was a seventeen-year-old boy named Ho Tzu-Hsin, a veteran of the Long March, who was assigned to Bethune as his houseboy and who remained with Bethune until his death. The other was his interpreter, Tung, without whom he would not have been able to communicate. With his lack of Chinese it is amazing he was able to be as constructive as he was. He was so busy and so occupied that conversation, for the year and a half he was in China, ceased to be part of his life—but for somebody who loved social occasions and civilized, and sometimes uncivilized, argument and discussion, this must have been an excruciating spiritual loss.

Bethune did manage to persuade General Nie, who had doubts, that a permanent model hospital should be quickly built. It was created out of a typical peasant compound in a matter of weeks; Bethune decorated the courtyard of the small compound with Chinese banners and Spanish Republican posters. At the ceremonial opening he told the troops it was "our hospital," which they had created together. He told them that they, the Chinese, had shown him how to be selfless, co-operative, and undaunted by great difficulties. And he hoped that he had been able to instruct them a little bit in the mastery of technique. In this way they could learn to control nature instead of being controlled by it. For every procedure there was a right way and a wrong way, and they must learn the right way. He told them it was their duty to make the patients happy, to give them the means to fight for their own health.

> There's an old saying in the English hospitals ... "A doctor must have the heart of a lion and the hand of a lady." That means he must be bold and courageous, strong quick and decisive yet gentle, kind and considerate. Constantly think of your patients and ask "Can I do more to help them?"
>
> One of the tasks of this hospital is to develop leaders and when I say leaders I am thinking of the whole army and the whole district from the big leaders at the so-called top to the little leaders at

the so-called bottom. But there is, in truth, no top and no bottom. That is a false conception. Our organization is not like a house—settled, static and still. It is like a globe—round, fluid, moving and dynamic. It is held together like a drop of water, by the cohesion and cooperation of its individual parts.... So, even though you need leaders now and will for a long time to come, you must begin to learn not to depend upon ... your leaders. Be a leader yourself, though you only lead yourself, for every leader starts by first leading himself.

Bethune left the model hospital after a few days because of the autumn offensive of the Japanese. He went a hundred miles west to Hebei Province. Right afterwards, the model hospital, together with the whole village, was destroyed by the Japanese troops. Bethune realized that General Nie had been right, that any permanent facility was a ready target for the Japanese. So he developed a mobile medical team, which could arrive in advance of battles. Bethune had trained his interpreter, Tung, as an anaesthetist, and on December 7 he wrote to General Nie describing how the unit was able to move behind the regiments in action to supply operative first aid. It seemed a fine thing to Bethune. He operated on seventy-one cases in forty hours with the aid of two assistants, Wang and Ya, whom he himself had trained. Wang donated three hundred centilitres of blood and continued to work for twelve hours; Tung had severe tonsillitis and a high fever but nevertheless administered over fifty anaesthetics. Bethune concluded that the mobile unit was successful: on average, patients were arriving at the unit within twenty-four hours of being wounded. "I regard this as satisfactory as can be expected under the circumstances, as the country is very mountainous and transportation as a result slow." He received one patient only seven hours after he had been wounded. He was pleased that one-third of all people operated on escaped without infection.

All the equipment was placed on three mules: the collapsible operating table, a full set of surgical instruments, anaesthetics, antiseptics, twenty-five wooden legs and arms. Bethune felt that even in the event of a spontaneous action, if there was use of the wireless, separate military units could be tightened up and the operating unit dispatched to meet the wounded on their way back to the rear. He acknowledged that he was sometimes impatient with the young "doctors" he had trained. They ranged in age from nineteen to twenty-two, and the nurses from fourteen to nineteen, but he noted that they worked very hard and were trying to be better. As for himself, he was glad of the hard work, but he was desperate for supplies. He wrote to Dr. Ma-Haide:

> I have not seen an English-language newspaper for over six months, with the exception of the Japan Advertiser of April 18th, left behind by the Japanese ... I have no radio. My isolation is complete. If I did not have enough work to fill 18 hours a day, I certainly would feel discontented.
>
> Will you do this for me? Just one thing! Send me three books a month, some newspapers and magazines, I won't ask you to write letters. I would like to know a few facts—"Is Roosevelt still President of the United States? Who is the Prime Minister of England? Is the Communist Party in power in France?" Some other facts would be welcome also—"What is the China Aid Council doing for China, for the 8th Route Army? How much money have they spent? Are they sending more doctors or technicians? Am I to have assistance? Am I to have the medical supplies I have been asking for for five months? I have exactly twenty-seven tubes of cat gut left and one-half

pound of carbolic acid. I have one knife and six artery forceps—all the rest I have distributed. There remains two and a half pounds of chloroform. After that is finished we will operate without anesthetics.... What is Ewen doing? What is Brown doing? What does America say? What does Canada say?

All the above would seem that I was complaining bitterly of my lot. On the contrary, I'm having a swell time!

In the space of two months in 1939, he cut his finger three times because he frequently had to operate without gloves.

He wrote to a friend in Canada:

I have not seen an English newspaper for eight months now. I receive mail about every two and a half months apart. So you can imagine my delight to receive your letters, especially as they give me important news of changes at home. I am very short of books, as I have read and re-read all I have a dozen times.

My life is pretty rough and sometimes tough as well. It reminds me of my early days, up in the

Northern bush. The village is like all other Chinese villages made of mud and stone, one-story houses in compounds. Three or four houses are enclosed in a compound facing each other. In the compound are pigs, dogs, donkeys, etc. Everything is filthy—the people, their houses etc. I have one house to myself. It has a brick oven running along a single room. In this I have my cot and table. I have made myself a tin stove in which is burnt coal and wood. The windows (one) are papered with white paper. The floor is packed mud, so are the walls.

But the country is mountainous and bare of trees except in the little valleys. Streams run in the valleys. They are now completely frozen over. There was an inch or so of snow in December, but that has gone in the January thaw.... The worst feature of the climate is the biting high winds that come down from the Gobi desert to the northwest. They blow up great whirling clouds of dust and snow.... The Japs are all around us.... Let me confess that on the first of the new year I had an attack of homesickness! Memories of New York, Montreal and Toronto!

In a four-month period their unit was involved in four battles. In one, they were nearly captured in a village by four hundred Japanese. Luckily, with ten minutes' warning, they were able to pack up and escape, the patients hidden in straw or carried on the backs of civilians. Nobody was taken prisoner. He wrote to the China Aid Council that

> everyone was satisfied that operations can be successfully performed by mobile operating units, only one or two miles from the front. Not only can they be performed there, but it is essential that they should be.

Then he inquired:

> Why, oh why are we not receiving more help from both China and abroad? Think of it! Two hundred thousand troops, two thousand five-hundred wounded always in hospital, over 1000 battles fought in the past year and only five Chinese graduate doctors, fifty Chinese untrained 'doctors' and one foreigner to do all this work.

Bethune was convinced that to attend to a guerrilla army

properly he would need to train more medical personnel, so he revived the idea of a model hospital where he could teach doctors and nurses. The medical unit was a guerrilla unit— it travelled by horseback and sometimes on foot. He knew he couldn't do this without raising funds and became determined to return to North America to do so. Undoubtedly his experience in raising money for the Spanish cause convinced him that if he threw himself into giving speeches he would rouse people's sympathies. Bethune realized that in the short term foreign medical units coming to China could be of help, but that the Chinese must be "educated to carry on after [any] foreign unit moves away. That to my mind is a test of its real worth."

He explained this in a letter to a friend.

> The work I'm trying to do is to take peasant boys and young workers and make doctors out of them. They can read and write and most have a knowledge of arithmetic. None of my doctors have ever been to college or university and none have ever been to a modern hospital (most of them have never been in any hospital) much less a medical school. With this material I must make doctors and nurses out of them, in six months for nurses

and one year for doctors. We have 2300 wounded in hospital all the time. These hospitals are merely the dirty, one-storey mud and stone houses in out of the way villages, set in deep valleys overhung by mountains, some of which are ten thousand feet high. We have over twenty of these hospitals in our region, which stretches from Pei Ping [Beijing] in the North to Tientsin in the East, South to Shi Chia Chuang, West to Tai Yuan. We are the most active partisan area in China and engaged in very severe guerrilla warfare all the time.... The war will be a long one. We want it to be protracted. We are planning on a war lasting at least ten years.

Bethune was certainly prescient in thinking the war would last ten years; not until October 1949 would the Communists under Mao Zedong take control of China. Better than any biographer could, he lays out the drama he was living in and his emotions. The following letter was written to Dr. John Barnwell, with whom he had shared a cottage at the Trudeau Sanatorium in the 1920s.

It's a fast life. I miss tremendously a comrade to whom I can talk, you know how fond I am of talking! I don't mind the conventional hardships—heat and bitter cold, dirt, lice, unvaried, unfamiliar food, walking in the mountains, no stoves, beds or baths. I find I can get along and operating as well in the dirty Buddhist temple with a 20ft. high statue of the impassive faced god staring over my shoulder as in a modern operating room with running water, nice green-glazed walls, electric lamps, and a thousand other accessories. To dress the wounded we have to climb up on the mud ovens—the k'angs—they have no mattresses, no sheets. They lie in their old stained uniforms, with their knapsacks as pillows, and one padded cotton blanket over them. They are grand. They certainly can take it....

I'm planning to return to Canada early next year. I must leave here sometime in November and go five hundred miles on foot over to Yan'an. From there by bus—I hope down through French Indo-China. Then boat to Hong Kong. Another boat (a freighter to Honolulu to avoid Japan) then another boat to San Francisco. I want to raise a guaranteed thousand dollars gold a month for my work here. I'm not getting it.

> They need me here. This is MY Region. I must come back.
>
> I dream of coffee, rare roast beef, of apple pie and ice-cream. Mirages of heavenly food. Books— are books still being written? Is music still being played? Do you dance, drink beer, look at pictures? What do clean white sheets in a soft bed feel like? Do women still love to be loved?
>
> How sad that, even to me once more, all these things may become accepted easily without wonder and amazement at my good fortune.

He realized that he had a great deal to do before he could leave, and he continued to work at a hectic pace. In November, while probing a wound with his fingers, he cut himself on a bone fragment. In none of his letters did he ever indicate that he was not in good health, but his immune system must have been severely compromised; blood poisoning quickly spread through his entire body. On November 11, 1939, he wrote his last letter.

> I came back from the front yesterday. It was no good my being there. I couldn't get out of bed or operate.... I think I have either septicaemia from

the gangrenous or typhus fever.... If my stomach settles down will return to Hua Pai hospital tomorrow. Very rough road over mountain pass ... I feel freely today. Pain over heart—water 120 to 130 degrees. Will see you tomorrow I expect.

Norman Bethune.

A few hours later, at twenty minutes past five in the morning of November 12, 1939, Norman Bethune died in a tiny hut in the village of Huang-Shih K'ou.

Both Ted Allan and the novelist Zhou Erfu report that Bethune had written a will. In it he tells General Nie that he is fatally ill and is going to die. He asks him to inform the China Aid Council. He asks also whether the council will aid his ex-wife, and he tells General Nie that he would like his English shoes to go to him and his riding boots and trousers to General Lu. He asks them to give his everlasting love to all his Canadian and American friends and says that he regrets only that he cannot do more. It concludes: "So the last two years have been the most significant, the most meaningful years of my life. Sometimes it has been lonely, but I have found my highest fulfillment here among my beloved comrades."

He loved the Chinese, and for them he did what he could. He could give no more. He had written "I am tired but I don't think I have been so happy for a long time. I am content. I am doing what I want to do." He ended his life in harmony with his convictions. In return, a billion and a half Chinese would come to know him as Bai Qiu En—The Light Who Pursues Kindness.

Seventy Years Later

I cannot finish this book without reflecting on two moments that have had a great impact on me.

In Yan'an two years ago, in 2007, I saw the whitewashed, Spartan room where Norman Bethune and Mao Zedong met in April 1938 and talked through the night. The square, high table, the two chairs, the k'ang-a ceramic stove that served as a bed platform, all matched the well-known poster. It has been kept almost exactly as it was, this provincial merchant's house—grand for a small town, but simple and almost bare. I felt the spirit of these two men—the bold, charismatic revolutionary leader who had led the Communists out of certain annihilation and saved them and himself; and the Canadian doctor, impatient to get going, to learn what he could do in this remote part of China to help these people fight fascism. The reality of that meeting and the consequences of it are still palpable in that room.

The other moment was in Ottawa, on October 20, 2001, when a fine monument was unveiled in Green Park on Sussex Drive to honour the veterans of the

Mackenzie-Papineau Battalion. At the time, I was Governor General and was deeply touched to see how many of our great veterans of the Second World War were there, including Colonel Cliff Chadderton, showing by their presence that the fight against fascism began in earnest in Spain in 1936 and continued until 1945 with the defeat of the Axis. I felt as if the story had come full circle.

SOURCES

Among the many books I consulted, a few that readers of this biography might find interesting are Roderick Stewart's *Bethune* (1973) and *The Mind of Norman Bethune* (1990), Larry Hannant's *The Politics of Passion: Norman Bethune's Writing and Art* (1998), Ted Allan and Sydney Gordon's *The Scalpel, The Sword* (1952), and Kathleen McCuaig's *The Weariness, the Fever and the Fret: The Campaign Against Tuberculosis in Canada, 1900–1950* (1999).

There is an equally broad selection of archives. Among the most useful to me were those of Norman Bethune, Roderick Stewart, and Hazen Sise. Most fruitful and revealing are the journals of Marian Dale Scott, which have never before been consulted to help shape a biography of Norman Bethune.

ACKNOWLEDGMENTS

Norman Bethune has inspired many writers, and I owe a great deal to their research and commitment. Most notable among them are Roderick Stewart, who continues to illuminate this subject and whose generosity is equal only to his grace, and Larry Hannant, who has made available so much of Bethune's art and writings, in a context that is invaluable. The writings of Mac Reynolds, Ted Allan and Sydney Gordon, Jean Ewen, and Michael Petrou have clarified much about Spain and China in the 1930s. The Chinese People's Foreign Affairs Institute was of great help and most hospitable on my research trip to China. I am particularly grateful to Ambassador Wang, Leon Lui, and all their representatives in Beijing, Shanghai, Xian, and Shijiazhuang. They showed me that the spirit of Bethune lives on. Thanks to Ann Scotton, Marian Dale Scott's literary executor, and P.K. Page for enlightenment. Ambassador Lu Shumin of the People's Republic of China to Canada gave unfailing support and encouragement. At the Osler Library Archives, Pamela Miller and Christopher Lyons were kind and thorough. At the Library and Archives Canada, special thanks to Ian Wilson, national archivist, for the lovely space and to Ilene McKenna for locating invaluable material. Thanks to Carlos Muñante and Ambassador Malcolm McKechnie at the Canadian Embassy in Spain, to Jonathan Weier for his excellent and frequently innovative research, and to Thomas Hodd for his great help, support, and patient good humour. Gratitude to Mark McConaghy for his help with Chinese transliteration, which has changed in the last seventy years; I have used familiar forms to aid the reader's comprehension. At Penguin, David Davidar is comfortingly imperturbable and Diane Turbide, firm and helpful. And thanks to Yvonne Hunter and Mary Opper. I am particularly grateful for the sensitivity and understanding of Alex Schultz. This series works because of all their talents. Gratitude to Michael Levine, friend and counsellor.

And my respect to John Ralston Saul for his diligence and my thanks for our continuing conversation.

1890   Norman Bethune is born on March 4 in Gravenhurst, Ontario.

1909–11   Bethune studies at the University of Toronto.

1911–12   He works in a lumber camp in northern Ontario.

1912–14   Bethune is a medical student at the University of Toronto and works at Frontier College.

1914   He enlists on September 8 with No. 2 Field Ambulance Army Medical Corps, serving as a stretcher-bearer.

1915   Bethune is wounded at Ypres on April 29; he spends six months in hospitals, mostly in England.

1915–16   He returns to his medical studies at the University of Toronto in an accelerated program.

1916   Bethune graduates in December with a Bachelor of Medicine, University of Toronto.

1917   He joins the navy as surgeon lieutenant on April 25 and serves aboard the aircraft carrier HMS *Pegasus* for fourteen months.

1919   Bethune holds an internship at the Great Ormond Street Hospital for Children, London, England, then engages in a medical practice at Ingersoll and Stratford, Ontario.

1922   He is elected a fellow of the Royal College of Physicians of Edinburgh on February 3.

1923   Bethune marries Frances Campbell Penney on August 13.

1924   He sets up practice in Detroit, Michigan, serving mostly working-class, immigrant patients.

1926   In the fall, Bethune is diagnosed as having tuberculosis. He leaves Detroit for the Calydor sanatorium, Gravenhurst. On December 16, Bethune is admitted to the Trudeau Sanatorium, Saranac Lake, N.Y. He and Frances separate.

1927   Bethune returns to the Trudeau Sanatorium; creates a mural, "TB's Progress." On October 24, Norman and Frances are divorced. On October 27, Bethune is given artificial pneumothorax treatment. By December 10, he recovers completely and is discharged from the Trudeau Sanatorium.

1928–32 In April, Bethune moves to Montreal to the Royal Victoria Hospital, the Medico-Surgical Pulmonary

Clinic. He specializes in thoracic surgery, teaches at McGill, and lectures and demonstrates at the Trudeau Sanatorium.

1929   After persuading her to rejoin him in Montreal, Norman and Frances are remarried on November 11.

1931   Bethune becomes associated with George Pilling and Sons, Philadelphia, manufacturers of medical equipment.

1932   In March, he serves as acting head, thoracic surgery, at Herman Kiefer Hospital, Detroit, for six months. Then Bethune is appointed to Sacré-Coeur hospital, Cartierville, Quebec, as chief of pulmonary surgery.

1933   Norman and Frances are divorced a second time on March 30.

1935   In June, Bethune is elected as council member of the American Association for Thoracic Surgery. In July, he sails to Britain en route to the International Physiological Congress in the Soviet Union and spends several days in London with Marian Dale Scott and her son, Peter. Bethune organizes the Montreal Group for the Security

of the People's Health in the fall and joins the
Communist Party of Canada in November. In
December, he helps organize and finance the
Montreal Children's Creative Art Centre.

1936   In July, the Montreal Group for the Security of the
People's Health issues a manifesto to candidates in
the 1936 Quebec election. Bethune volunteers for
medical work in Spain in September, leaving
Canada on October 24, 1936, under the auspices
of the Canadian Committee to Aid Spanish
Democracy. Bethune spends the next two months
travelling and organizing a blood transfusion service for the front lines with Henning Sorensen and
Hazen Sise. On December 12, the Canadian Blood
Transfusion Service begins operations.

1936–37 Bethune conducts several radio broadcasts from
Spain to stimulate help for the Republican cause.

1937   Bethune's blood transfusion team helps to transport some of the hundred and fifty thousand
refugees to Almería after the evacuation of Málaga
on February 7. On April 19, Bethune submits his
official resignation as the head of the transfusion
unit, which is taken over by the Spanish Ministry

of War. Toronto gives Bethune a triumphant homecoming on June 14, followed by a similar event in Montreal.

1938   On January 8, Bethune sails from Vancouver for Hong Kong with the Canadian-American Medical Unit to China. From February 22 to March 22, he makes the long trek to Xian from Hankou. Bethune meets Mao Zedong in Yan'an on March 31. In June, he arrives in Chin-Ch'a-Chi region and becomes medical adviser to the Eighth Route Army.

1939   Bethune celebrates his forty-ninth birthday on March 4. On October 28, he is called to the front because of heavy fighting; he nicks his finger while operating on a soldier and contracts blood poisoning. On November 12, Bethune dies in the village of Huang-shih K'ou, Hebei Province, China. Mao Zedong's Tribute to Norman Bethune appears on December 21, 1939.

1952   Bethune's remains are moved to the Martyrs' Tombs at Shijiazhuang three yars after Mao Zedong's victory.

1971   Canada recognizes the People's Republic of China with an exchange of ambassadors.

1976   A Norman Bethune statue is unveiled at
       Dorchester and Guy streets in Montreal.

1995   On November 28, the Parliament of Spain unani-
       mously offers Spanish citizenship to all veterans of
       the International Brigades, including the
       Mackenzie-Papineau Battalion.

2000   In July, a Norman Bethune statue is unveiled in
       Gravenhurst, Ontario.

2004   In May, Málaga, Spain, names a street for Norman
       Bethune.

2005   The Red Cross Technical Training Centre of
       Almayate, Spain, is named for Norman Bethune.

2006   El Paseo de los Canadienses, a two-kilometre
       promenade by the sea where the refugees fled in
       Málaga, Spain, is inaugurated "in memory of aid
       provided by the Canadian people from the hands
       of Norman Bethune to the fugitives in February,
       1937."